GW00994883

Dr Mc

Lou a

Chitialhann

27 8·05

REALIZE WHAT YOU ARE:
THE DYNAMICS OF JAIN MEDITATION

REALIZE WHAT YOU ARE:

THE DYNAMICS OF JAIN MEDITATION

BY

Gurudev Shree Chitrabhanu

Edited by Leonard M. Marks

Drawings by Jeffrey R. Webb

DODD, MEAD & COMPANY

NEW YORK

Copyright © 1978 by Jain Meditation International Center, Inc.

All rights reserved

No part of this book may be reproduced in any form
without permission in writing from the publisher

Printed in the United States of America

1 2 3 4 5 6 7 8 9 10

Library of Congress Cataloging in Publication Data

————

Realize what you are.

Includes index.
1. Meditation. 2. Self-realization. 3. Jainism. I. Marks, Leonard M.
II. Title
BL1378.6.C47   294.4'4'3   78-9461
ISBN 0-396-07579-7

CONTENTS

THE IMMORTAL SONG

May the sacred stream of amity flow forever in my heart,
May the universe prosper, such is my cherished desire;
May my heart sing with ecstasy at the sight of the virtuous,
And may my life be an offering at their feet.
May my heart bleed at the sight of the wretched, the cruel,
and the poor,
And may tears of compassion flow from my eyes;
May I always be there to show the path to the pathless
wanderers of life,
Yet if they should not hearken to me, may I bide patiently,
May the spirit of goodwill enter into all our hearts,
May we all sing together the immortal song of brotherhood,
The immortal song of sisterhood,
The immortal song of brotherhood. . . .

—CHITRABHANU

EDITOR'S
INTRODUCTION

This book is intended to introduce the West to Jain meditation, a system of meditation which has been practiced in the East for more than 2,500 years. The book was compiled and edited from extemporaneous talks given before various American audiences by Gurudev Shree Chitrabhanu on the fundamentals and philosophy of Jain meditation.

Gurudev Shree Chitrabhanu

Born in 1922, in Rajasthan, India, Gurudev took the vows of a Jain monk at the age of twenty, having been inspired by his father, who later joined him as a monk, and Mahatma Gandhi, with whom he worked for Indian freedom. The first five years of his monastic life were spent mostly in silence and meditation. Gurudev spent twenty-nine years as a monk. During that time he walked over 30,000 miles barefoot across India in an effort to bring people from all points of view beyond narrow sectarianism while encouraging them to experience self-realization and seek the highest and best in themselves through meditation.

After becoming one of the spiritual leaders of India's four million Jains, Gurudev founded the Divine Knowledge Society in Bombay and other social welfare and emergency relief organizations which work among the poor and distribute food, clothing, and medicine. He accepted invitations from the Temple of Understanding to address the first three Spiritual Summit Conferences in Calcutta in 1969, in Geneva in 1970, and at Harvard Divinity School in 1971. By his decision to attend these conferences, Gurudev broke the 2,500 year old tradition prohibiting travel by vehicle and became the first Jain monk to travel outside of India. Gurudev subsequently made lecture tours in Europe and Africa and later accepted many invitations to teach in the United States. In 1971, Gurudev gave up the monastic life and his position of authority in order to carry his universal message beyond India. In the United States he has worked closely with the Temple of Understanding and has lectured at the United Nations, Princeton, Sarah Lawrence, Cornell, the State University of New York, and many other institutions of learning and human development. He is closely associated with individuals and students involved in yoga, psychiatry, philosophy, government, business and the arts. At present, he is spiritual advisor to the Jain Meditation International Center in New York City and to centers directed by his students in Pittsburgh, Boston, Palm Beach, and Boulder as well as in Brazil and India.

The Jain Meditation System

The methods of Jain meditation described in this book are universal and intended for anyone interested in expanding his or her awareness. This form of meditation goes far beyond those schools of "instant" meditation which appear to be the current fad. Jain meditation does not rely on any secret rituals or mantras for which students are charged exorbitant fees. Jain meditation does not involve mechanical repetition of meaningless sounds. It does not promise students occult or psychic powers. The goal of Jain meditation is not solely relaxation, although relaxation is one of the obvious benefits that flow from its practice. Jain meditation works on far deeper levels. It is attuned to modern psychology and seeks to encourage us to overcome negativity, to erase and replace conditioning and influences which have not allowed us to fulfill our potential. It stresses the gradual development of twenty-four hour awareness in addition to the recommended twenty-four minute period of meditation. Finally, Jain meditation is designed for us to experience ourselves in the deepest spiritual sense. The aim is to go beyond mere words and concepts, to realize what is permanent in ourselves, and to approach the world from that central reality.

A Thumbnail Sketch of Jainism

Readers may be interested in a thumbnail sketch of the essence of Jain tradition from which Gurudev comes, although this is not necessary for understanding or practicing the meditation in this book.

Jain is derived from the word "jina," a person who conquers his inner enemies and brings out his highest qualities. According to Jain philosophy, Adinath was the founder of Jainism. Modern Jainism is based upon the teachings of Bhagwan Mahavira, the twenty-fourth and last Tirthankara or prophet of Jainism, who was born in 598 B.C. Jainism rests on four main principles:

1. Non-violence, *ahimsa*—in its broadest sense, including non-violence not only in actions but also in speech and thought.

2. Relativity in thinking, *anekantwad*—the belief that there is no one truth, but rather that truth has many aspects which are represented by different standpoints.

3. Non-acquisition, *aparigraha*—the principle of limiting possessions and requirements, including avoiding the possessive attachment of other people as well as material goods.

4. The law of deeds or actions, *karma*—which states that we are all responsible for our own past words, thoughts and deeds and that we each may shape our own futures with positive thought and action.

The Organization of This Book

The first five chapters of this book are extemporaneous talks given by Gurudev at the Jain Meditation International Center in New York on the fundamentals of Jain meditation. This is a five-week course which has been successfully given to many students to introduce them to the basic practice of Jain meditation. It is recommended that

the reader spend one week practicing the methods out-
lined in each chapter before moving on to those described
in the next chapter. While the instructions are easy to follow, the practice takes gradual effort and concentration.
The four additional chapters are based on talks given by
Gurudev concerning the philosophy of meditation and its
role in our daily lives. Chapter VI is based on a talk by
Gurudev given at the Chicago Yoga Conference in June,
1976. Chapter VII is a talk by Gurudev at sunset in Central
Park in June 1974, as the final lecture in a series sponsored
by the Universalist Church of New York City. Chapter
VIII is a talk given at Wainwright House in Rye, New
York, in May, 1974. The final chapter is one of a series of
talks on the philosophy of soul and matter given by Gurudev in 1977 at the Jain Meditation International Center in
New York.

I am indebted to many friends at the Jain Meditation
International Center for their help and encouragement on
this project. Thanks are due to June Fog (Janaki), John
and Lyssa Miller, Rick Kleifgen (Rakesh), Howard Banow
(Abhai), Clare Rosenfield (Brahmi) and especially to my
wife, Sara. Our hope, in the words of Thomas Merton, is
that this book will help us "to become what we already
are."

Leonard M. Marks

Gurudev Shree Chitrabhanu

CHAPTER

I

What Is Meditation?

From time immemorial man has been in search of his hidden powers. He knows intuitively that there is more in life than what he is now experiencing. His deepest longing is to discover that which is more, that hidden power, and to bring that power into action to make this life as happy, peaceful and creative as possible.

There are many means and ways to embark on this journey but I have found one thing common to all philosophies, faiths and teachings—meditation. Meditation is at the heart of all religions: Hinduism, Jainism, Buddhism, Judaism, Christianity, Taoism or Zoroastrianism. This universality of meditation points toward the great potentiality and power it can tap. Meditation opens the door to higher consciousness where our treasure is hidden. Our real Self is buried inside; our strength is slumbering.

With the help of meditation you discover your inner potentiality. You explore that area which is untrodden and

1

untouched. You reach that core of peace where tranquillity resides. In meditation you reach the summit of joy and bliss. You find that there is nothing in the world which can compare with that blissful peak moment.

Who will find these beautiful experiences, if not human beings? Only as human beings can we reach this height of tranquillity. There comes a moment when we experience the universe as our home. Then we transcend any feeling that the universe is a hostile place where we do not naturally belong. With the help of meditation, we come home and settle into our own real Self. Now we are not at home; we are all in separate houses. You know the difference between a house and a home. Houses are made of bricks; homes are made of feelings. When you have a guest, you use the expression "Feel at home"; but are you really at home with yourself?

When you meditate, you find your own real home, inside yourself. When you learn to experience this, outside things do not disturb you as they do now. You develop the power to keep them out. You do not allow them to disturb your peace. You discover a castle inside where you are safe from all attacks. This is the whole idea of meditation. Meditation is not a religion; it is a means of learning the art of living, growing and communicating.

Now you are very vulnerable, easily hurt and upset. One person can make you laugh, another person can make you cry. One can make you dance, another can put you down. You may think you are independent, but you are reacting to somebody else's words, emotions, actions and reactions. You don't know when you will weep or laugh, be elated or depressed. Can you truthfully say now: "It is up to me how I react to the acts of the world. I have balance. I know how to live with myself"?

Each of you has a vast reservoir of energy. In fact, you *are* that energy which reveals consciousness. In meditation, you unlock this energy so you can grow. You begin to feel confident and happy. Now you may become nervous over a small thing like a job interview. But why do you worry? What can the interviewer do to you? He or she is a human being like you; once he or she came for an interview also. With this attitude you can go calmly and enjoy a conversation with that person or anyone else.

When you maintain this awareness and this way of thinking, you break barriers which you have erected. Slowly you realize that what was possible for any person in history is also possible for you. You are also in the line of history. You belong to the same species. You share the same energy, the same source, the same light. The only difference is that some have developed their full potentiality and others have not. Some have realized their strength to do so, and others have not.

In meditation we come from the circumference of our lives to our center. Each of us is an individual world. We act and interact with each other. We form relationships. The definition of a relationship is this action and interaction between two worlds. So far we have had time for everyone else—our children, our husband or wife, our boss, our colleagues and friends—but we have not taken time for the one who is working for all of these people. These people are on the circumference. At the center there is one who pays attention to all. We *are* this center. Meditation means becoming aware of this center. It is finding our strength, this reservoir of energy, our inner treasure, our own Self.

Now you may have control over your body, but you don't have control over your mind. When you begin to meditate you will be surprised and shocked to know that your mind is not under your control. Your car, your children, your office staff may be under your control, but your own mind is not. You won't be able to focus your attention for five minutes on one thing. In five minutes you will go mentally to five different places, or ten or twenty. This demonstrates that your mind is not harmonious. If your body were as uncontrolled as your mind, you would not be able to cross the street. At least when we want to cross the street we can coordinate ourselves and go there. But when we tell our mind to do something, it will immediately do something else.

In my school days I had a teacher who would say to one of the students in the middle of class, "When the class is over, please buy me some vegetables so on my way home I won't have to go to market." One day I said to him, "We are here in school, and yet you are thinking of home and sending us to buy vegetables." He said, "Yes, and at home I am planning your lessons and thinking of you here in school." He was a good example of how the mind works. In school he thought of his home. At home he thought of the school.

Look at yourself and see if this does not apply to you. When you are home with your family, don't you think of business and plan for the things you must do the next day?

And at the office don't you think of problems at home, of your spouse and children, and of things you would rather be doing than the task at hand? This also shows your mind lacks control. The incessant jumping of your mind consumes your energy and misdirects it. When you are not acting with awareness, your energy is going in another direction. Sometimes you do not use even a fraction of your energy. That is why you make mistakes in driving, typing, writing, calculating, or in talking to people without focusing on your words or their impact.

These errors will be minimized by learning to concentrate and by bringing the power of your whole mind to a subject. When you are talking to someone but thinking of something else, you may use harsh or wrong words. Later you say, "I'm sorry, I did not mean it that way." But if you did not mean it, why did you say it? Nobody was forcing you to say the wrong words or use the harsh tone of voice. Your apology may erase some of the pain, but it cannot erase everything. Some spot remains. It is like the typewriter: we may erase and type the correct letter five times, but still a reader can see that some error was made.

Meditation is used to educate our mind. This is basic. An uneducated mind is as dangerous as a high-speed automobile with weak brakes. It can create disaster at any moment. What we learned in school was formulas, information, repetition. That was a different thing. What we are now seeking to learn is the art of living. In training our mind we change the quality of our thinking from negative to positive. Then we know how to use all our information properly, precisely and effectively.

Beginning Practice

Now that we know some of the benefits to be gained from meditation, how do we begin to practice?

Your Place

First, find a quiet corner in your house where you can meditate. Make it a plain and simple place with a little fresh air and very little noise. Pick a spot where you feel relaxed and comfortable. To avoid distractions many people just use a simple wall in their meditation spot. Or you may want to place a beautiful picture there, or a graceful vase with a single flower, or another inspiring image. Any arrangement or painting should be symmetrical and peace-giving. Modern paintings which are distorted or very stimulating may be good at other times, but not during meditation. The picture reflects on the brain cells and they pick up what is in front of you. That is why the statues in temples are so beautiful and peaceful, with serene faces and sweet smiles. They create an atmosphere of peace, as you should do in choosing your place for meditation.

Your Time

Next, select one special time each day for your meditation. It may be in the morning, in the afternoon or in the evening; it does not matter what time of day as long as you have time for yourself and no other duties to perform just then so that you will not be disturbed. If you are busy with other things when you meditate, your mind will be loaded or bombarded with all your obligations. So make a peaceful time for yourself. Decide that you are entitled to twenty-four minutes a day just for you. Aren't you entitled to allow yourself one minute of peace for each hour of the day? If you feel that it is absolutely impossible for you to find twenty-four minutes for yourself in a day, this does not suggest that meditation is not for you, but that meditation is a *necessity* for you. If your priorities are so arranged that you cannot carve out a brief period each day to come to yourself, your priorities need reordering.

You may give the rest of the day to your family, your friends, your business or your work, but give the gift of this time for meditation to yourself. It is a time to be with yourself. Forget about what you gain or don't gain. This thought itself creates tension and there can be no attention when there is tension. Give freely to yourself this gift of time and remind yourself that for this twenty-four minutes you have nothing to do. These are a few minutes of leisure and pleasure, simply to feel what you feel inside.

If you choose the same time every day to meditate, your body will gradually adjust to this new schedule. If you enjoy a cup of coffee every day at three o'clock, then you will begin to feel sleepy as that time approaches. Your body is reminding you to have your coffee. Our body's reactions are nothing but a series of habits. It will adjust itself to any new habit we form. Nothing is impossible. Some things may be difficult and may take time, but with awareness and persistence, any new pattern can be formed. Then your body will be your friend and it will even remind you each day that your time for meditation has arrived.

Your Posture

Now we have a pleasant place and the right time for meditation; the next thing we need is a good posture. If you can sit in the lotus pose, that is excellent, but do not feel embarrassed or inadequate if you cannot. If your joints become sore and painful, you will be distracted and you will give up before long. The lotus position has become famous because in India the people do not usually sit in chairs. There is very little furniture in most homes and so from childhood onward the people sit on the floor. Their bodies are conditioned in this way, and if they were made to sit on a chair, they would become stiff and uncomfortable. The beauty of the lotus pose is that it keeps the spine erect, but it is not compulsory for meditation.

You may sit in a chair or on the floor with your back against a wall, or you may even try lying down. The two main things to remember in the posture you choose are to have your back straight and to be relaxed and comfortable. The spine is a beautiful column of energy. It is an electric line, and all the energy from toe to head passes through that line. If you know how to keep the spine straight and strong, you will reduce the risk of disease. That is why the aspirants sleep on a harder surface, to keep the spine from being bent in sleep. This helps to keep you healthy and gives longevity and an impressive appearance.

If you see someone sitting, standing or walking with

a slumping posture, you do not think so much of him. Those who are standing straight and tall naturally please our eye and impress us. Once you have the habit of being straight, then you will always walk and sit with your head up. No feeling of depression or lowliness will come over you. The world is nothing but your reflection. Your posture reflects you.

The spine is also very important in digestion. When the spine is straight, all the organs are held in place and our system is kept in order. When we slump over, the digestive organs are squashed and the blood supply is not as good and fresh. How can digestion be good when our internal organs are under this kind of pressure? Constipation results from not eating properly and from not keeping the spine straight.

Another benefit of sitting with the spine erect is that our breath can go deep into our lungs. Shallow breath hurts the body and makes us feel sluggish and drowsy. When we breathe in naturally and properly, the air goes deep into our body and the diaphragm expands so that the abdomen is pushed out. Then the navel goes back in when we exhale. Breathing in this way we feel alert and calm. You will notice when someone becomes angry or passionate, their breath is very rapid and shallow. In depression and emotional disturbances we see quick and jagged breathing. But when you are in meditation or thinking a beautiful thought, you feel calmness and the breath is very slow and deep.

Experiencing this, we realize how important the breath is to our mind and thinking, to our peace and calm. When we breathe properly, we won't have fatigue or depression. The body will receive the proper oxygen supply and flow of blood, and disease will not be able to take root. To enjoy proper breathing, we must have good posture.

If you now have any problem with your back or your digestion, you can alleviate it by sitting straight, breathing properly and concentrating on health and vitality. A story illustrates this point.

It was noticed that a prince's spine was not growing straight. All the court doctors were summoned and it was agreed that unless some treatment was devised, the child would become a hunchback.

This news greatly disturbed the king, who sent out word throughout the land that a large reward would be paid to anyone who could cure his son of the curvature of his spine. From that day on, a steady stream of doctors, nurses, scientists, healers, magicians and other sorts poured into the palace with every imaginable herb, root, exercise, potion and incantation. None of the methods improved the boy in any way.

Finally a wise sculptor who knew the art of meditation heard of the poor child's problem and came to the king. He asked only for some sculpting supplies and materials and the chance to spend three days with the boy. However, he warned the king that it had taken a long time for the condition to reach this stage, and they must allow time for it to disappear. The treatment would take two years.

For two days the wise sculptor worked on a composition, carefully studying the boy's physique from many angles. During this time no one was allowed to see the piece. Finally the third day came and the sculpture was unveiled. It was a perfect statue of the boy standing straight and tall.

Then the sculptor explained the method of treatment. Each day the boy was to go before the statue and stand in exactly the same upright pose for as long as he could without strain or pain. He was to imitate exactly the posture of the statue, including the dignified and regal look the figure had on its face and the way it held its head.

The sculptor explained that if the prince did as he was told, his spine would straighten and his posture would be excellent. The prince agreed to try and the king was encouraged, although his advisors told him he was crazy.

The sculptor spent the third day with the boy explaining that as he stood before the statue he must think of himself growing straight and tall and taking the shape of the figure before him. Each day while standing he was to visualize himself in his mind's eye as becoming straight and tall like the statue. The most important thing to remember, the Master told the boy, was not ever to miss a single day. To be certain, he should do his standing the first thing in the morning when his mind was clear and fresh, before anyone's glance or remark could remind him of his hunched condition.

The boy was then eight years old. On the fourth day the Master left the king's palace with no reward. He said that he would return in two years to collect the reward, after the treatment had been proven. The boy kept up the practice of standing before the figure each morning very early before anyone else in the house was up and around.

Each day he felt himself growing stronger and saw himself growing taller and straighter. Each day he felt better and better and his confidence improved. Those who were living around him and saw him every day did not notice any change at first but then they began to see it also. First they noticed that the boy's attitude was changing, that he was happier and more sure of himself. Then they saw the change in his body begin.

When the wise sculptor returned two years later, the boy was the picture of health. He cut a truly regal figure, standing as straight and tall as any boy in the entire kingdom. His father was overjoyed and offered to give the Master anything he desired. The joy of seeing the boy in health and strength was reward enough for the wise man and he left as quickly and quietly as he had arrived.

This example gives a glimpse of the power of meditation, our own inner power to change the conditions of life.

Beginning Meditation: Calming Down and Observing Yourself and Your Breathing

Now you have selected a quiet spot, a peaceful time and a relaxing posture for meditation. Next close your eyes and watch yourself. See yourself with your mental eye. You may think, "What should I do with myself?" Then you may feel silly and think, "What am I doing here? Why am I sitting here like this, doing nothing?" You will think of all the projects and chores you want to finish—the bank, the groceries, the party, the job, the appointment—all will come into your mind now. It is natural because your mind is always engaged in some activity. If you have nothing else to do, you turn on the radio and begin chewing gum. People go to the seashore and into the mountains, to nature's most serene and beautiful spots, carrying their radios and chomping their gum. You may know what to do with people and things, but you do not know what to do with yourself.

First, just sit and let your own thoughts come. What kinds of thoughts appear? How many kinds are there? What fancies and silly notions come to mind? See what tendencies and instincts are hidden in you. The first step is to sit and watch, to discover the habits and tendencies of your body. Watch as a neutral observor. Don't think of anything as bad or good, as right or wrong; stay judgment-free. Remember any adjective that any person has used for you is not here now. If someone has said you are ugly, leave it behind you. If someone has said he or she doesn't like you, let it go for now. Begin to see that you are beautiful. Begin to feel a pleasant feeling within yourself. Let this feeling come over your face. Visualize it soothing and relaxing you. Visualize yourself sitting for meditation with a pleasant, peaceful expression.

You may now see all of your needs arise. Ask yourself, "Why do I have them? What are my desires? How do they manifest themselves?" From these questions you gain insight. Is there some pain which is disturbing you in your subconscious? Unnoticed or unnecessary nervous actions, like tapping your foot or biting a fingernail or smoking a cigarette, reveal your discontent or pain.

Because of anger and hatred, frustration and resent-

ment, we become tense and ugly. Through meditation
we are rebuilding ourselves. We bring the power of our
mind to build new cells in our face and our whole body.
If you watch your face in meditation for one year, making it happy and smiling and presenting a good image to
yourself in your inner eye, then a change will come in you
and everyone will notice it. People will wonder what
cosmetic you are using, but the real cosmetic is meditation.
You will change yourself if you believe in yourself.

In life, what you conceive, you receive. What you
think, you become. Now our life is out of our control because we feel sorry for ourselves and do not sincerely
want to take the steps to change. We only *wish* we could
change. But a wish has no strength, no backbone. A wish
is wishy-washy. We must use our will instead. Don't allow
any doubt to counteract your will. Otherwise one thought
will simply cancel another and you will go nowhere. A
negative thought is a weed that can spoil the garden of
your heart and mind.

Once I knew a man who had a large house and a
beautiful lawn and garden. Each morning he would wake
up refreshed, go out and sit in his garden and meditate.
He would look over the grass and plants and seek out any
weeds. If he saw an unwanted weed growing anywhere in
the place he would bring his attention on that spot and
concentrate. The man's gardener was very sensitive; he
would then see the weed and go remove it. Then the man
would scan the lawn again and find another weed. Bringing his attention to focus on it, the gardener would then
see it and take it out. In this way the man kept his lawn

and garden and all the grounds of his home beautiful. In our meditation we are doing the same thing.

Now as you are sitting and seeing your face in a beautiful light, you may notice some skin problems. Why do you worry about it? It is the sign of the bubbling energy of youth, of your inner heat and strength. Do not be negative about it; eat the proper food and watch as it goes away.

Next direct each part of your body to relax, working upward slowly from your toes to your head. Make your jaw relaxed as you sit. We release any tension because the tension which we store in our bodies makes us unattractive and drives away our friends. Friendly faces are beautiful because they are natural and sweet-smiling. No one notices whether their features are well shaped or in proportion because love flows from them. Now in meditation you are creating a new face and a new feeling. After you relax your jaw, relax your whole face, around the eyes and mouth and in your cheeks, taking away all frowns, grimaces and scowls.

Now you become calm and concentrate on your breath. Breathe only through your nose, not your mouth. Watch your breathing and, without controlling it, see how the breath comes and goes.

Our breath comes and goes in three levels, as you can observe. First it comes into the chest area; this is the shallowest part. Then the ribs expand as we draw the air deeper into our body. Finally the diaphragm expands, causing the stomach to distend. Be aware of each of these three parts to your breathing as you sit in meditation.

Feel your body filling with fresh energy as you inhale. Then allow the breath to go out of your body and feel that you are removing any tension or fatigue or negativity as you exhale. In this way you rejuvenate yourself with every breath.

Spend the first two or three days observing these bodily needs and tendencies. Take your time with yourself. This is not a race or contest. After this period you will be ready for the second phase of this practice—bringing the mind to one-pointedness.

Developing One-Pointedness

Sit and watch inside until you feel comfortable, quiet and calm. With your eyes still closed, imagine a beautiful flame in the center of your brow. It is a clear yellow-white flame sprouting upward. It is exactly at the center of your brow. See it there.

If this is easy for you to see, make this practice part of your meditation and continue to do it every day.

Some people find this visual imagery difficult. If you do not see the flame, or if it will not come easily into your imagination, then light a real candle and set it at eye level in front of you. This is best to do in a darkened room. The background behind the candle should be very plain. Sit and watch the candle for two minutes. Now close your eyes and visualize the beautiful flame coming in the center of your brow. Relax and bring it inside you. If you have difficulty, open your eyes and look at the candle for a short while again. Do this two or three times for a few moments each time, but no more than that. Be very careful not to strain or overexert your eyes.

The candle is a beautiful symbol of ourselves. The wax is like our body. The flame is our real Self, our soul or spirit. What happens if we turn a candle upside down? We see that the flame turns upward. The flame will never remain downward no matter what you do to the wax. Your body is like this beautiful candle and *you,* that which is the center, are like the flame. The wax melts but the flame moves upward. Though our body ages, *we* remain the same. Visualize this symbol. Don't identify with changes in the color of your hair or wrinkles in your skin. We can slow this process down, but we can never stop it. Nature must work on our body; it is the nature of the body, and the nature of nature. The body is only the circumference, like the candle melting and changing its size and shape. At the center is you, which, like the flame, does not change.

For the first week, relaxation and concentration are your lessons. Relax your body, watching its needs. Observe your mind's vagaries and fancies. Then concentrate on this flame, remembering its deep meaning. This meditation will give you an understanding of your center. With an understanding of your center, you will then learn how to command the circumference.

Questions

1. Should we concentrate on our body and thoughts for twenty-four minutes or on the flame?

First make the decision that you will sit for twenty-four minutes. Resolve to remain for the full time. Then watch your body as it wants to move about. See your restlessness and your habits and fancies. When anything comes into your mind, speak to it as you would to a child you love. Say "Now I have some work to do so please leave me alone for awhile. I will have some time for you later, but not right now." Gently come back to your concentration.

For the first two or three days, do only this. Then add the visualization of the candle flame for the rest of the week.

2. Should we do this once a day?

Yes, to start with, once each day is fine. Later, if you choose to, you can do it twice and then increase the length of time. But now, one time is enough.

3. What is the best time of the day?

When your stomach is light is the best time to meditate.

4. When I first tried this method, I had this problem—first the image of the candle kept changing and it was very unsteady, as if it were being blown by the wind. Then it caught something on fire and I had a forest fire beginning in my mind. . . . Should I try to keep this from happening? How?

Don't try to suddenly curb or stop your thoughts. Watch them first and see the tendencies of your mind and imagination. Be patient with yourself. Bring yourself back to the image of the steady flame. But be aware and see the shapes, designs, colors and everything. See the power of the imagination and go beyond it.

5. What if I get sleepy?

Meditation helps you to drop tension. You really don't fall asleep but you lose awareness of your body. This is called *yoganidra,* the sleep which comes from yoga and meditation. It is a very wonderful state. Einstein once said that when he had "direct experience of silence" for a few minutes, he was more rested than if he had slept for five hours. Sometimes people sleep for eight hours, but they are always chasing others and doing business in their dreams, so they are more tired when they wake up than when they went to sleep. This meditation will make you calm so you will have the best kind of rest each night.

CHAPTER

II

Deepening Meditation: Emptying and Focusing

Once a well-known professor visited a famous master of meditation. As they began to talk, tea was prepared and when it came the master began pouring in the professor's cup. He poured and poured until the cup overflowed and still he continued pouring. Finally the professor could not resist, and he said, "What are you doing? The tea has overflowed the cup but still you keep on pouring! Why do you keep trying to put more in when there is no room left in the cup?" The master replied, "Yes, my friend, you are right. Your mind is like this teacup. It is filled to the brim with opinions and prejudices, dogma and theology, logic and arguments. Whatever I pour into it now will overflow. There is no room left for anything to enter. Unless you empty your mind, what can I give you?"

In Eastern countries this anecdote is often used for beginners who are interested in meditation. When the students come, the teacher tells this story very early in their training. Meditation is not meant to add to what is already in your mind. If we add fresh things to what is polluted, the fresh things will become stale and foul along with the old things. So we must empty ourselves or we will be unable to feel the freshness of the new learning we receive.

Meditation has three main connotations. The first is to see a thing properly and clearly, as it is. When we have difficulty in school, the teacher tells us to concentrate and meditate on the problem, to bring our complete attention to the subject matter and see it clearly. In this way we find a solution. The second aspect of meditation is to perceive that which is behind the thing you are seeing, to go beyond the superficial world. It is like the husk and the grain. In our normal way of thinking and seeing, we are aware of only the husk. But there is grain on the inside, beneath the husk, and it is the grain which is rich and nourishing and full of energy. In meditation we go beyond the husk and find the grain of life. The third aspect of meditation is to concentrate on only one thing at a time. You learn to train your mind to do only one thing and leave the other duties and obligations for another time. In this way you do not waste energy in fantasy or being somewhere else; you bring your full awareness to the one thing before you at the moment. Doing this in each moment you feel a flow in life. You accomplish many more things each day in a more precise manner.

This beautiful example illustrates the power of meditation very well. One of the greatest scientists in India, C. Raman, received the Nobel Prize for his work in science. At a large gathering in his honor, he told the elite of the nation this story when they asked him to speak.

"What I have achieved," he said, "is the result of meditation and a lesson my father gave me. When I was a young boy of ten, my father came to me with a magnifying glass in his hand and he said, 'Come with me.' It was summer and we went into the garden where he collected a few blades of grass and made a heap of them. Then he asked me, 'Do you think that the sun can burn these blades of grass?'

"I thought for a moment and answered, 'No, I don't think so. The sun is not burning anything now and I don't see how it could start burning this little pile of grass.'

"Then he said, 'Let me show you.' He held the magnifying glass over the grass so the sun's rays could pass through it. In a short time the little pile burst into flames.

"Then my father told me, 'The same sun was shining here on all the earth, but it did not ignite the blades of grass. Now see the miracle. I brought all the rays together through this magnifying glass and they became power, energy, fire. The scattered rays of the sun will not ignite the grass, but when they are brought together, focused on one point, they create energy and fire.'

"Then my father told me, 'If you want to have any success in life, to achieve anything, you must bring all your thoughts together. You must have one-pointedness. Then you will know there is not anything in the world in which you will not succeed. Success does not belong to any special people, nor to any special race, caste, creed or sex. Success belongs to those people who can bring their whole attention to one-pointedness. If you focus on anything, it will open its heart to you.

"'Now I am not going to tell you anything more,' my father continued. 'I am not going to tell you what job you should do or how you should live your life. Keep this magnifying glass with you as a teacher, and go in life and work in any field. But remember to concentrate on whatever you do.'

"This glass I am still carrying with me and the Nobel Prize which I received is the result of this lesson in concentration."

In that way C. Raman ended his short address to the most highly educated people of the nation. This is a beautiful parable for our growth. Each of you wants to have some kind of growth, some achievement, some mission. Meditation helps you first to find and see your mission and then to fulfill it. It helps you by focusing the energy which is now being used in many different directions.

Without a mission, life has no meaning. It is only eating, drinking, sleeping and surviving; an animal can do those things. The purpose of meditation according to the saints and seers is to perfect human life, to open us to the higher levels of consciousness. Then the question comes, "What is the meaning of this term, 'higher levels of consciousness,' and how many kinds of consciousness are there?"

Wherever you see the movement of feeling, there is consciousness. Even in an ant or a leaf, there is consciousness. If you add water or pour acid on the plant, it will respond according to what is received. If you try to catch an ant with a piece of paper, immediately it will change its direction and try to get away. A fly will also avoid you quite skillfully whenever you try to capture it. Somehow they know there is danger and they move away to preserve their lives. Even bats who cannot see are able to perceive danger and escape. All living things possess a kind of consciousness. Birds migrate and fly without any map or chart. We may get lost trying to take the expressway to New Jersey, but they fly thousands of miles every summer and winter. This is instinctive consciousness and it helps them survive and find food and shelter. This is the first level of consciousness.

Impediments to Growth: The Ego

Next we come to the human being, who is conscious of himself or herself. The birds and animals do not have this quality. When anything threatens or disturbs animals, they are ready for either fight or flight. We are different. We do not fight only for food or clothes or shelter, but for something else; we fight for our ego's needs, the feeling that "I am something," the drive for power and subtle types of greed. This tendency does not leave even the holy men, the rishis, seers, saints, yogis and munis. This is the food of the most intelligent, ambitious, creative people.

My teacher used to say that the most difficult thing
to give up was not sex, or pleasure, money, the home or
even family. Beyond all these, there still remains ego and
the power drive. This is the primary hurdle for spiritual
growth. When this ego comes over us, when the ambition
and need for power come over us, they daze and dazzle
us. Other people wonder why a person changes in this
way, but they don't see that the person is under the spell
of the ego and that he or she is not aware of himself or
herself. It is as though they have drunk alcohol; they
lose their sense of balance spiritually, and they fall down
and utter meaningless words.

The ego is a very subtle form of intoxication. It is
very difficult to cross and go beyond. It is a thin veil
whose nature is opaque; sometimes we may see through
it to the other side and we know we are being held back
by it, but still we cannot go beyond it.

The deeper meaning of meditation is to overcome
the ego which holds us back and makes us miserable.
Even within a family, between husband and wife, parents
and children, when ego makes people take a stand, they
won't budge an inch. When ego comes, love departs. In
its wisdom, love will never remain in the presence of
ego; it leaves immediately, saying, "You finish first. Then
I shall return." You must decide what you shall give up,
ego or love. When the thought "I am something" comes,
then ask, "What am I?"

In order to advance you must break with the old pat-
terns. Do not worry about what others may say or how they
may judge you. George Bernard Shaw had three lines of

response when people told him of his critics' words. "What do they say? Do they say that? Let them say it!" With this simple reply he would free himself of all concern over petty criticism. In meditation we stop collecting the opinions of others. Instead we obtain direct insight into ourselves. Whether we receive a compliment or harsh criticism, we do not become upset because we understand that we know ourselves better than anyone else can.

Once a man became angry at the Buddha because his son had decided to leave the family business and live a spiritual life. He went to the spot where Buddha was seated quietly in meditation and began screaming at him. The more he shouted the more angry the poor man became, until he had abused the Master for more than an hour. Finally the man became exhausted and fell silent. Then the Buddha calmly replied, "If a man came to you and offered you a bucket filled with jagged rocks, would you want them?" The man shook his head, a puzzled look spreading over his face. Then the Master continued, "And if he tried to give them to you anyway, would you take them?" Again the man shook his head. "Then where would the sharp-edged stones remain?" asked the Buddha. "With the fool who brought them to me," answered the man, indignant at being asked such a simple question. The Buddha then said, "That is what has just occurred, my friend. You have brought me your cutting angry words, but I do not want them and so I have not accepted what you offered. Now they remain with you."

This kind of awareness is the real achievement. Outer achievements are only ephemeral. Our own growth in understanding and inner strength is far more rewarding than the superficial praise of passing strangers.

Techniques are like a tugboat. They take the ship out to sea and then their work is finished. The ship goes on into the deeper waters. In the same way, meditation techniques help us to go within and begin our voyage on the ocean of consciousness. If our mind is anchored by ego or we want to keep it stowed away in some safe harbor, then no technique or method will be able to launch us on our way.

Continuing Practice: Meditation on *Hrim* and Breathing

Last week we meditated on the light of a candle flame seen in our third eye, directly at the center and slightly above the two brows. Now we shall meditate on "hrim," a word first used by Jain saints in 850 B.C., the time of Parshvanath, one of the twenty-four Prophets of the Jain teaching. Along with this word there is a technique which is used to raise energy along the spine to the top of the head. When we do this, we experience pleasant vibrations and good feelings in our nerves and in the cells of our brain. With this experience of vibrations, our mind becomes in tune with the higher energy, the energy of universal consciousness, which is the meaning of the word "hrim." Using this special method of repeating the ancient word "hrim," we begin to move into the realm of our Higher Self and expand our consciousness.

In our spine we have many blocks which have kept us from experiencing our full energy. Now we shall feel some vibrations which will activate our slumbering dormant energy. Everybody has energy but it is slumbering. The lion is asleep. If it is awake, then no one can oppose it, but when the lion is sleeping, a mouse can play on its belly. The people who did great things were just like us, but they awakened their energy. When the energy is awakened, then you become a master in your field. If you are an artist, then you paint beautifully. If you are a composer, then you compose beautiful harmonies and melodies. If you are a poet, beautiful verses will come. If you are a person with awareness, then human insight increases. All this energy lies dormant, waiting within us. So now we want to stir that energy and bring it to our use.

To start, sit comfortably, either in the lotus pose, in a chair, or in the posture selected by you earlier. The main beauty of the lotus posture is that the spine remains very straight, but it is not compulsory for meditation. Begin to feel your breath. As you inhale, go along with your breath. For this work, you must yoke your ego consciousness and gradually limit the mind's constant activity. Yoga means to yoke. Here you yoke your mind to focus on the breath. As you inhale, let the breath go very deep to the voicebox, to the heart, to the navel, to the pelvis, and to the very last point of the vertebrae. Let the incoming breath go as far as you have spinal nerves. As you exhale, watch your breath and go along with it. Your ego consciousness will become very busy with your breath. Go and come as the breath goes and comes. Engage your ego for this task as you would use an employee in your work.

Now begin to count the breaths. As you inhale, mentally count one and as you exhale, count two. Then inhale while counting three and exhale on four. When you finish counting to four, begin again, starting at one as you inhale.

Now practice this for four or five minutes: first just watching your breath come and go, then counting your breaths.

In this way you become in tune with your life force and you begin seeing your inner world. Your senses, which are always busy and racing, occupied with unwanted things, stop when you feel your breath and do this counting. It keeps your mind busy because if it leaves the work, you miss the count.

Now we come to the vibrations of "hrim." It is important that we learn to pronounce this word accurately because if we do not, later it will gradually change more and more and we will be saying a different word with an entirely different meaning.

The "h" in "hrim" is not like an English "h," which is very soft and often hardly pronounced at all. In Sanskrit "h" is a much heavier sound, like "huh." When you speak it, you contract your stomach muscles and feel a throb in the area of your navel. The sudden contraction in the navel and the exhalation helps to lift your energy upward.

The energy we speak of is called "kundalini" energy or "coiled" energy. According to the Eastern teaching and tradition, at the base of the spine near our sexual organs we have coiled energy. When this energy is used for generation, it gives momentary joy and pleasure. The teaching is that it should be lifted upward instead of always letting it go downward and out through the sex organs. The "huh" sound at the beginning of "hrim" gives this energy an upward thrust and helps to lift it. The "huh" is like a propellant for this energy.

As we inhale to begin this technique, we feel our breath touching five spots or energy centers in our body. First we feel it at the throat, and then we feel it move to the heart, the navel, the pelvis, and the very base of the spine. In each spot we feel it for only one or two passing seconds and then we move on. The inhalation is one smooth flow; our awareness stops briefly at each spot. We may do the inhalation to a mental count of ten. When the breath reaches the bottom of our vertebrae, we hold the breath for a few seconds. Then we begin "hrim." As we make this sound, we feel the energy coming up along the spine. The "huh" sound gets the flow of energy started and we feel the vibrations of "r" and "i" briefly as the energy moves toward the top of the head. Then as it rises toward the head and brain, we feel the humming vibrations of the "m-m-m" sound, especially at the top of the crown of the head. The breath passes out through the nostrils, touching the third eye between our brows.

The humming of the "m" is a sound like the gentle buzzing of a bee. For this reason, this technique is sometimes given the name "Buzzing of the Bee." In your mind's eye you can visualize your brain and the top of your head as a beautiful white lotus flower with innumerable petals. As the energy is raised along the spine to the head, the flower opens and the sound becomes that of

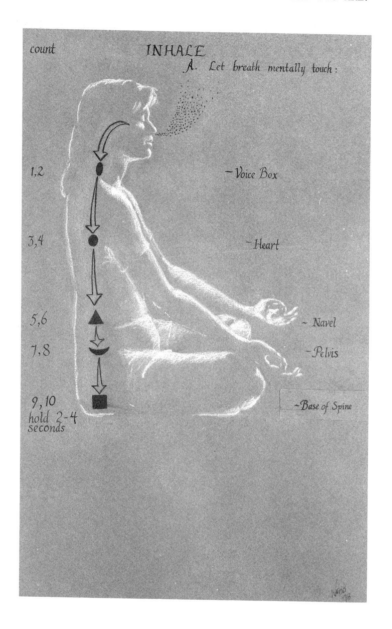

count   INHALE
                         A. Let breath mentally touch:

1,2   – Voice Box

3,4   – Heart

5,6   – Navel

7,8   – Pelvis

9,10
hold 2-4   – Base of Spine
seconds

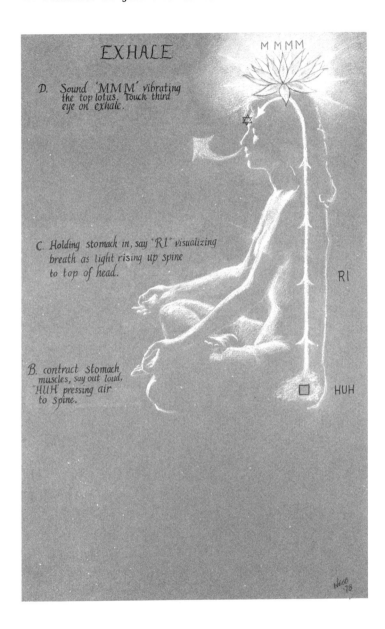

EXHALE

M M M M

D. Sound 'MM M' vibrating the top lotus. Touch third eye on exhale.

C. Holding stomach in, say "RI" visualizing breath as light rising up spine to top of head.

RI

B. contract stomach muscles, say out loud, 'HUH' pressing air to spine.

HUH

a gentle bee hovering in the air above the nectar of this sweet flower. In this way you can feel and see your own energy as it is lifted. Feel the vibrations as if giving a massage to the brain nerves. It feels very nice. Now practice doing "hrim" aloud several times.

You can begin to feel calmness and peace. Eventually, as your practice continues over days or weeks, there comes a calm moment when you lose track of your ego-self. You don't know where you are. In that moment the inner door opens and you are universal. Ego consciousness drops away and that higher intelligence which has been hidden is revealed. Meditation is the means to see this and go higher. You realize the oneness of yourself and the universe, of your energy and universal energy. The desire for happiness and the repulsion to unhappiness is the same in all people as it is in you. Experiencing this oneness, this unity of universal consciousness through meditation, we can change our life and make it more positive and thoughtful. Now, burdened by the ego, we only think in ego terms. We see everything in relation to *our* benefit and *our* need. Lifting our energy and going higher, we see differently. We see the good in others, not just what they can do for us. It is this clearer vision which can bring peace to us and through us to mankind.

With this universal sight, creativity surges out. When the ego and the small self leave, the power of creativity comes forth. Any creative act or performance is only appealing when the actor or musician forgets his or her ego and becomes "lost" in the performance, intoxicated in the Higher Self. Otherwise, it may please our ears but it can never touch our soul. All great scientists and artists were in touch with the flow of this creative energy when they made their finest discoveries and designed their masterpieces. In the same way, you must "lose" yourself in order to find your true Higher Self.

This week, sit in a good posture in a place where it is comfortable and quiet and where there is some fresh air. Watch your breath and then count your breaths—one, two, three, four. Then do the "hrim" exercise three times. Afterward you may sit quietly in meditation or you may focus on the light of the candle flame at your third eye. You will see that your meditation will become very pleasant because the energy has been lifted upward. Your energy is going to the crown center at the top of your head and you become very peaceful.

Questions

1. You say "hrim" out loud when you are meditating, right?

    Yes.
2. May my wife and I meditate together?

    You can do it together. That is beautiful.
3. How do we know when to start?

    It is a good question. Take about two seconds to touch each of the energy centers as you inhale. One can say "inhale" and then both of you can inhale while mentally counting to ten and then holding the breath for a four count together. At first you may have different timing but soon you will synchronize your pace.
4. Is it beneficial to try to inhale as long as possible and exhale as long as possible?

Yes, but one thing should be remembered: tension should not be created. Increase the depth of your breathing slowly and the lungs will become strong gradually and naturally.

5. I am curious about something. When you meditate yourself, do you use many different techniques or is there one you do all the time?

I use the techniques we teach in meditating with you, but the aim is to make your entire life a continuing meditation. So whether I sit for meditation or not, I am always in a meditative mood. I am always in tune with meditation. At first, for two or three years, we must practice, but ultimately we become aware even when we eat and drink and talk. We are always there in our center. This is the ultimate goal, to feel and be one with all. And we learn the lessons of life, that in whatever we do we should be positive and nothing we do should become negative or harmful to ourselves or anyone else.

6. How many times a day should we practice?

Two times if it is possible. If it is not possible, once every day.

7. Now, first we are to feel the breath and then count it. And then we do "hrim" three times. Does that take most of the twenty-four minutes?

No. You do a little breathing and counting and then pause and do "hrim." Then you sit for meditation. This practice is conducive to meditation.

8. Then meditate on the flame?

Yes, the flame or you may choose the point of light at the third eye.

CHAPTER

III

How Shall We Approach Life Through Meditation?

This whole universe is an open field for man's growth, happiness, awareness and enlightenment. Still, human beings are not receiving from the universe even a portion of what they are capable of receiving. Why? Because they have limited themselves, put up a fence composed of their perceptions and beliefs. They receive according to these perceptions and limitations. Meditation breaks down the fence; it lifts the curtain which is created by society and the skeptical mind. You start experiencing the reality that "The world is for me and I am for the world. If I am open to the world, the world is open to me."

This experience is like visiting your mother's house. There you can go and feel at home. You can eat anything you want anytime. Your mother will not be angry to see you going to the refrigerator. She will be happy to see you enjoying the food she has prepared for you. This earth is like that mother, but your doubt, guilt and fear have caused you to lose your relationship with her. You are afraid to reach out, afraid you will be rejected, rebuked or put down. You do not spread your hand or extend yourself to receive those gifts the universe can give you. With meditation you are opening yourself. That is the purpose of meditation. When you open, things naturally flow in and you receive.

If we open a window, the air comes in. We don't have to ask or call the wind, all we must do is open the window. If we open all the windows, we have cross-ventilation and the air comes and goes freely. You do not worry that the wind will escape and you will be left without any air. More wind is always coming so we enjoy the breeze. It is infinite, everlasting. Some people fear that by giving they will reduce their own supply. But the universe works in a different way. By opening to give and receive, there is never any lack or want. We receive the flow of air from higher consciousness through the open windows of our mind. Our fears are created by our mind. What you think will come to pass. If you think something bad will happen and dwell on it, then you invite that event and naturally it comes about. That is the law of the universe.

Meditation means to send an invitation to health before the subconscious mind can invite weakness and sickness. There are beautiful things happening in the universe, but often we don't enjoy them. The world is not as bad as the newspapers, television and radio indicate. They report abnormal events, the unusual and unpleasant. Do the papers ever report how many people went home safely and happily? They do not, because this is what is normal and usual and people do not read about these things.

In our lives we must clear the clouds and see the beauty and positive energy all around us. Then our whole approach to living changes. Now our subconscious mind is busy with unpleasant, negative, petty things. They cover our smile, cloud our happiness, blur our vision, upset our mood. Life is not upset by big things; they come only rarely. It is the tiny irritations which disturb our lives. If a small incident occurs in your family and you become irritated, it can spoil your whole day. A little ink will ruin your clothes. It takes no time to spoil something but much time to clean it up. People are not ready to take the time to find out why they are unhappy and irritated, or why they lose control of themselves. Meditation means taking that time.

Why do you need to take this time? For years you have been conditioned by your society and its rules, by your teachers and schools, by your parents, your religion, even by the climate and geography of the place where you live. You have been covered by many layers. You have forgotten your real nature which is serene and happy. You need to take time to rediscover your real nature.

There is an old fable which shows what has happened to many of you. Once there was a wise king who ruled his kingdom well. One day his minister came to him and told the king that he had had a dream that the water of the next monsoon would cause all the people who drank it to go crazy. The king became very concerned. So he decided to cover the palace from the rain so that someone

in the land would remain sane and capable of ruling.
This was done. When the monsoon started and the people began to drink the water, they began to feel light-
headed and then they went completely crazy. They all began taking off their clothes and walking about naked in
the streets.

After one or two days the king decided to make an
appearance before the people and tell them not to worry,
that a solution would soon be found to their problems.
And so he set the time and appeared on the balcony with
his minister. But when the people saw him, they all began
to shout at him. They talked among themselves and decided that the king must be crazy because he was still
wearing his clothes. Then they decided that they should
lock both the king and his minister away in a safe place
until they regained their sanity and were again able to
govern intelligently. When the king heard this he knew
what he had to do. Both he and his minister quickly removed their clothes and threw them away. The people all
began to cheer and applaud, and they settled down to
listen to the speech of their king.

The same thing has happened to you. You have been
conditioned for many years to think that you are weak
and worthless inside. Instead of seeing joy in life through
your own eyes, you have accepted the negative vision of
others.

If your mind believes that you are worthless, then no
one else can convince you that you are priceless. Now we
have all taken a step toward meditation to understand
what we really are, to leave these old concepts of guilt and

sin behind. Once we get a glimpse of our real Self, then our lives will be changed and we can free ourselves from the conditioning of others. We will see that life is worth living.

With the help of meditation, we learn and grow from each experience in life, from happy incidents and painful events, from richness and poverty, from gaining a place in society and from being rejected by society and friends. We use meditation to draw wisdom and to grow. We do not allow any moment of depression to cover us or make us feel helpless. We stand up and say, "With my suffering I have paid my debt. Now I am free. Let me move on and leave it behind." With that thought you rise up and move onward on your path.

Once I knew a very lovely and sweet young woman who was about to have her first baby. Suddenly her husband died. The poor woman faced a terrible struggle because she did not want to live without her husband, yet she had another life to consider. She took it as her mission to live for this second life, this unborn child, and to raise the child to the best of her ability. Taking this mission, she used her suffering and hardship to learn and grow and to strengthen herself to give to those around her. She meditated on her child and saw the child's needs. She felt, "I live for thee." With this feeling, living is not mere existence; living becomes *life*.

Ask yourself, "Do I learn and grow from my experiences? If I do not, then what is the meaning of living?" When you go to the store and buy some costly items, you return home without as much money. But you do not feel disappointed because you have used the money to get something you wanted. This is also the way we invest our days. We are passing time here; we want to spend our days learning and gaining wisdom, understanding and balance.

If life goes by and you have not attained anything which is real, then old age is miserable. If you have never known yourself, then the prospect of dying and the approaching time of departure are very frightening. But if you know yourself and grow in life, then advancing age is beautiful; each stage of life holds new richness and rewards.

We do not grow old, we become old. To grow means to increase our wisdom and vitality. Years are not important, it is pleasantness that counts. I have seen many beautiful old faces, people in their seventies and eighties who are so wonderful to look upon. Though there are wrinkles, in each line some pleasantness is hidden. And I have seen young faces which are dull and flat and covered with powder. There is no pleasantness to be found there. The flat faces are good for portraits and magazines, but not for communication. Meditation means that you bring a pleasant feeling in your face. You see beautiful moments from every corner of your memory. Bring those moments to your memory now so your face becomes pleasant and peaceful. When we become tired of life we become old, whatever our age may be. Meditation is useful for older people as well as the young. As we advance through life meditating, we build our good feelings and joy.

The first thing to know about meditation is that you must start from here, wherever you are now. Once a lady was walking out of her house and she dropped her ring near the doorway. It was very dark there, so she walked a few yards and began looking around under the street-lamp. A man came along and asked her what she was looking for. When she told him she had dropped her ring, he began helping her look for it. After a few minutes, he asked her exactly where she had dropped it. Then she explained that she had dropped it near the doorway, but because there was more light under the streetlamp, she was looking for it in that spot. Then the man said, "You cannot expect to find the ring here just because there is light. You must go to the spot where you dropped the ring and bring light there if it is too dark."

The same thing is true for us in our meditation. Each of us is at a different point from everyone else; not better or worse, just different. It may seem that your spot is rather dark at first, but you cannot find what you are looking for anywhere else. You must bring the light of your increasing awareness where you are in order to begin your quest. There is no comparison in this journey. You simply start from where *you* are.

The first step is to become calm and observe your feelings. See yourself in your relation with the universe. Are you alone in the world? Do you feel alienation? Why? Do you feel that you do not have any friends? Or is it that you do not have anyone who satisfies *your* desires? We can view life in two ways: in the large context of the whole universe, or from our little self and its connection with endless desires. Seeing the world the second way, though many people smile and say "hello" to you, if *your* desires are not exactly fulfilled nothing will be right for you.

Now, take some time to examine your needs. Consider the people who have no food, no clothes, no shelter; or the aged who sit in corners all alone, their hands trembling, with no one to bring them water. Consider the young who are innocent of any crime except to be born in a certain country at a certain time, and are forced into a battlefield against their will. If they refuse to go, they are branded as traitors. If they ask, "Why should we fight?" or say "I have no enemy; they did nothing to me and I did nothing to them," they lose their freedom and are locked in jail. If they go, they must kill and many will lose their lives in hopeless struggle.

Do you not see that you are blessed? Why do you yearn for what your mind desires? If things come, that is fine. If they do not, why do you let it spoil all that you already have? See the blessings you have. Do you have a good body with five beautiful senses? Can you walk, talk and communicate? Can you see, hear and think?

Come in touch with this beautiful body. It is a gift of the universe and it plays a great role in our growth. Use it well and don't abuse it. Build it in strength and health.

First count your gifts. Then ask yourself, "Do I have any relation with the universe?" With a little thought you will see that the answer is *yes*. The food you eat is grown by someone, though you may never meet him. The clothes you wear were made by others you never see. And what about your house, the car you drive, the electricity you use? Could you create all this by yourself? Thinking in this way you will see that you have a vast relation with the universe and you are constantly receiving its plentiful gifts. Realizing this, you feel rapport with all mankind and you want to dedicate yourself to the good of the universe.

Continuing Practice

We sit and feel our breath as it comes and goes. As we become calm, we begin to count—one as we inhale, two as we exhale, three as we inhale again, and four as we exhale. This helps to settle our metabolism.

Then we will encounter our mind, which is always busy running. Our thoughts are like the cars moving in the street, and before we begin our meditation there is a great traffic jam within our mind. It is rush hour and hundreds of thoughts are moving through our mind at once. Meditation means to allow this jam-up to clear. We don't add new thoughts now. Instead we sit and wait and watch, gradually becoming the calm spectator of this internal flow. Then we can see what is hidden in our subconscious.

The Use of Mantras: *Veerum* and *Sohum*

If we have difficulty slowing our thinking process, we can begin to use a mantram. In Sanskrit, *man* means mind and *tra* means to control or lead. We bring control over our mind by using a *mantram*. The mind is like a monkey, jumping from one branch to another. If we tell it not to jump around, it will go even faster. It is like a child: if you tell it not to do something, immediately it starts doing that thing even more. If you sit to meditate and try not to think, the mind will find a million topics to think over. To quiet the monkey, we give it a banana. Then it stops to eat and becomes calm. A mantram is like a banana which we give to the monkey-mind so it will become quiet and peaceful. We give it this word or phrase to work on, to keep it busy and happy.

But a mantram is also more than this. The mantras we use are words which are filled with a deep meaning and pregnant with universal energy. They were originally used by the saints and seers of ancient times, thousands of years ago, and they have a great significance in lifting our thoughts and inspiring our lives.

One mantram we can use is *veerum,* which means "brave amongst the brave." As we repeat the word, we feel its meaning deep within ourselves. "I am the brave amongst the brave." We see the challenge of life and we are not afraid. We accept life as an adventure.

There are three levels on which we can use this mantram. First you may want to articulate *veerum,* to say it aloud and feel the vibrations around you. When your mind is very active or you have been in a noisy congested place like a subway or in traffic, you can say the word out loud to clear your mind of harsh sounds. Creating these sound vibrations will soothe you and bring calmness.

Going to the next level, you feel the word on your

breath as you inhale and exhale, creating silent vibrations without saying *veerum* aloud. You feel *vee* as you inhale and *rum* as you exhale. In this way, you feel a rhythm in your breathing and deep peace in your mind. You can prolong the *vee,* taking a deep inhalation and you will see that your circulation will become calm and harmonious. Slowly and gradually your heartbeats will slow down because tension has dropped away. You feel a relaxed mood come over you. You mentally think of this word as you feel it on your breath.

Then you go to the third level and glide into your center. It is very near sleep, but it is not sleep. In this very deep state of meditation, your center opens to you. Here insights come and sometimes premonitions and mystical experiences. Here, in the real Self, the whole treasure is waiting for you to see.

We are like travellers on a dark and foggy night. We can't see where we are going and there is confusion and misunderstanding. We sometimes feel very lost. Then insight comes—it is like a flash of lightning in the night. For a moment the horizon is illumined. Then darkness returns, but what has been seen cannot be erased. In the same way, in that moment of the experience of reality you are different, you are not any name or form. You are aware of what you really are. You are pure energy. In this way the mantram takes you into your pure real Self.

Let the mantram play on your breath, feeling *vee* as you inhale and *rum* as you exhale. Allowing the breath to come and go, you feel the ebb and flow of the universe. You are no longer afraid of anything for there is nothing to lose. Life is continuously coming and going. Something comes in one hand and goes out the other. We stop clinging because we see that clinging ultimately brings suffocation and death. Your body and your breath are changed with these vibrations of *veerum.* The mantram begins to vibrate in all your activities. At your job, in your family relations, or just relaxing quietly, the subtle sound rings at the back of your mind. You remember and feel that you are as brave as any of the bravest souls.

There is another deep and powerful mantram you can use in a similar way. That is *sohum.* You inhale on *so* and exhale on *hum,* as with *veerum. So* means "that" and *hum* means "I" or "this." "That" and "this" are not really separate. It may appear that "this" is here and "that" is there, but that is only the appearance of separateness. Everything is in relation to everything else. If there is no "that," there can be no "this": and without "this," "that" could not exist. *So* is dynamic energy; *hum* is magnetic energy. *So* is sky and *hum* is earth. *So* and *hum* are all the poles of our existence brought into unity and harmony. *So* is God, the universe, the divine, the Higher Self, the real Self. *Hum* is this human being, the microcosm, the subconscious, the accumulation of thought and the mind. *Hum* is form and *so* is formless.

When you use *sohum* regularly, you are changing or altering your consciousness. That which was commonplace becomes meaningful. Going deep, you are aware not only of your body and mind, but of your indestructible energy. You are not perishable. You were, you are, you will be; this you experience in meditation. Form in this life is always changing, but at the center of all form is the changeless. We can see this center in all the forms. For example, look at pictures of yourself in infancy, childhood, youth and today. On careful reflection you will realize that you are still that essence which was within the changing forms in all the pictures. Then you know, "I was. I am. I will be."

If you experience this changelessness, you will always know that "I am here." We must break our fear of annihilation, of losing our self. This fear goes very deep in our mind. When you truly know "I am," then you realize "I will be" and "I can do." On the inside you feel the passive "I am," and on the outside you experience the active "I can do."

When you have that experience, then you no longer are concerned with inferiority or superiority. Seeing all life, you know you are equal to all, even the greatest Masters, the sages and the Enlightened Ones. You must go beyond the intellectual level, beyond words and concepts, to *real* experience; then you break the barriers between the saints and yourself and you become their friend. If we do not believe, we cannot receive. One who continues to live in a gutter cannot become the companion of one who lives in a palace. If we think we are nothing, if we feel helpless and weak, then the distance between ourselves and God will remain.

I remember one story which illustrates this feeling of unity. One night a young man went to pay a visit to his lover. It was very late so he climbed a tree near her window and called out softly to her. She heard him and asked, "Who is it?" He replied, "It is I, Calipha. I have come to visit you." But the girl answered, "Go away. There is no room here for you."

The young man was an aspirant and so he went to a nearby grove of trees and there he sat in meditation, pondering what might have caused his lover to respond in this way. After a while he had a flash of insight and returned. Again he climbed the tree and called to her. Again she asked, "Who is it?" Then he smiled and said, "It is a being. Just being." The door was then opened to him.

What did he see in his meditation? He saw that he had gone to her with adjectives and nouns, he did not go as essence. Thus he was an outsider. When he dropped the description and the outer concern and became in tune with inner reality, then there was no separation and she was waiting to welcome him.

This story is an example of what we are doing with ourselves in meditating on *sohum*. We are opening the door to our own higher consciousness, bringing union, breaking the separation between the inside and the outside, the interior and the exterior. This is the meaning of *sohum*.

So can also mean truth. We are meditating that "I am truth." Truth is not something borrowed from outside. Truth comes from within us; it is our real nature.

So also means love. We are repeating "I am love" as we repeat the mantram *sohum*. We do not cultivate love from the outside, it is a wellspring, always flowing from within us.

In this way we use this mantram to bring harmony and oneness in life. We feel this unity and we do not put God in a temple or a church far away. George Bernard Shaw once said, "Beware of the man whose God is in heaven." When God is in the distance, then man can do anything without interference. But when we see and experience God inside ourselves, there is no separation, no duality. That animating divine spark is everywhere, vibrating in every cell of our body. Without it we could not live for one second. As you inhale feel *so,* and as you exhale feel *hum.* Your breath begins to flow in rhythm. The vibrations build and you feel oneness. Repeat the mantram silently. There is no need to articulate it. Feel it, experience it, and be in tune with yourself.

Reaching this stage of meditation, you begin to live with joy, creatively and adventurously. Each day you see how you can test yourself. Each morning you think that you will create a new day for yourself. Regardless of the weather, you will create and sustain an inner climate. If the day is properly used, you find real satisfaction when you again come to meditation in the evening. Then you observe and see how the day was invested. You will not pass a single day without awareness if you practice this meditation.

In this way meditation slowly changes your life. You come from dazzling outer light into the cool moonlight atmosphere inside, from the active outer world to the receptive inner kingdom where there is peace and stillness. We are taking a journey with "sohum," gliding ever inward to our essence where we shall find the blessings of the universe.

CHAPTER

IV

Seeking Our True Nature

Meditation is a means to experience the music of the trinity of head, heart and hand. If these three are in unity, life becomes a symphony played by an orchestra and we enjoy living. But when there is disorder and discord, even though we try, life has no harmony or joy. When an orchestra plays, first the musicians tune themselves with each other. They train themselves to harmonize and each player gives ear to the other musicians. Each adjusts his instrument according to the others and then really joyful music flows. A beautiful symphony can be produced only if there is balance and harmony. If these instruments can become animated in the hands of the musicians and produce such uplifting music, think what an animated life can be produced when our five senses are in balance. With the help of meditation, we bring body, mind and spirit together; we seek the connection between the tone and the time. This lifetime can create

an immortal symphony which will bring harmony and
bliss to yourself and the people around you.

Meditation does not mean you go away and hide, or
withdraw from life to be a hermit and avoid responsi-
bility. Meditation is unity and harmony. The meaning
of meditation is to be with life. If you are eating a piece
of bread, enjoy it. Don't compare yourself with people
eating delicacies in the Waldorf Astoria. Only when your
mind is with *you* are you happy. When the mind goes
somewhere else, unhappiness is created. We start looking
down on ourselves. We imagine that life is working out
well for rich men, or politicians, or famous personalities.
It is always working out well for someone else, but not
for us. Even in a peaceful moment, the mind steps in to
tell us we are wretched.

Thinking this way, we ultimately become afraid of
happiness, afraid of joy and bliss. We believe the joy of
life is meant for others—the great saints and enlightened
men; that others must be gifted with some outside light
and energy. We think, "I don't have that gift, it is not
for me." And if it comes, we withdraw, thinking that
enlightenment is not meant for us; joy is not meant for
us. Believing this, it will never come to you. Even if it
does, you withdraw from it, you don't enjoy it. But if
someone tells you a certain teacher is enlightened, you
run to hear and see him. You believe enlightenment can
come to everyone but yourself.

The whole society lives in this way and some religious
teachings emphasize this way of thinking. For example,
many traditions put women in second or third class. The

priests have always been men, women could not carry the message. In some ceremonies women are not allowed to touch the vessels. Why? It is the deep guilt and feeling of sin, the idea that sex is unclean and evil. We are taught we are guilty of what is called "original sin." For thousands of years these kinds of thoughts have been hammered and nailed into our minds. You may try to come out of it, but it is in the air, on the radio on Sunday morning. It is deep in our minds, so it is very difficult to get away from it.

Eventually, we lose respect for ourselves, and we come to fear joy, bliss and enlightenment. Recently one of our students was meditating very deeply for many days. Going deeper and deeper, there came a moment when he began experiencing bliss and a deep merging with himself. Bliss was engulfing him, it was embracing him, and all the tension and fear and sadness were melting. Then the fear of bliss overcame him. He was so shocked that he got up and said, "No, I don't want this." It was a unique experience. He thought, "No, I am not ready."

In meditation there is a new moment, a new learning. The learning is this: you realize that all these beautiful things which you see in someone else are your privilege too. You are equal to them. It is not only Christ, the Son of God, or Mahavira, the Blessed Prince. It is not only Buddha, the Enlightened One. We all have the same potential. Again and again you must tell yourself that happiness, bliss and immortality are your birthright.

It is like the story of the musk deer. It has a gland at its navel which secretes musk and gives an enchanting scent. Catching its own smell in the air, the deer begins to run, seeking the source. Eventually it runs blindly into the desert, where it is very hot and there is no water. Its quest drives it into the wilderness where it becomes exhausted and dies. The musk deer has a life of tragedy. It does not die naturally, but dies in this fruitless search. The poor creature never finds peace because it never realizes that he himself is the source of the thing he desires most.

We all have this quest, but luckily we are human beings. Our lives need not be tragic. We can discover that the beauty we seek lies within ourselves.

To have this desire, this quest to know ourselves, shows we have the real quality inside. A chair or brick does not feel this desire or quest; it has no divine animating quality. But this special quality in us has been covered by many layers of opinions and conditioning. Meditation helps us remove the layers which have covered our nature. In meditation we are not *doing* anything or going anywhere. We are only removing the layers so our true nature can unfold and blossom.

The life of happiness is so strong and powerful that we must prepare ourselves to be ready to receive it. Our body, our mind, our soul must all be made ready. If you don't have money in the bank and you try to write a check for $1,000, you may wear a smile and pretend you are not bothered, but inside you know you are lying and cheating someone. It is not what is on the outside that really matters, it is what is inside.

In meditation we sit and watch ourselves and see how

many times we have to pretend, we have to feel big and important, or we have to act holy. It may be painful to watch if you want people to show respect and admiration or you want people to say, "Oh, you are a very special person, you are very spiritual and high." Then you will smile a little and say, "Yes, I am practicing spirituality." Inside you know how angry you are, how jealous you are and how competitive you are. Outwardly you pretend to be holy. In meditation, sit and watch, say to yourself, "What game am I playing? How am I pretending?"

As long as pretension remains, the truth will not dawn. Truth is not an abstract word, it points to what is real in life. When you accept real life, you may say, "I don't wear the mask of a smile. I am angry, you must know." Or you may say, "I still have many, many desires to be something, to make a show of myself and be in the spotlight. I acknowledge that I have this background. But I am striving to free myself from these shackles, from these chains of my past."

Sincerely and seriously you accept yourself. Don't try to collect opinions and praise for yourself. The more praise you hear, the more you have to pretend. You have to keep yourself to that standard, and it is a very difficult task because people build great expectations. They say, "You are a good person. You are very calm, you have no desires, you are above all these things." Then you have to cover your faults so people can't see them and you can obtain more praise. When you meditate, you are not creating any split personality, you are becoming genuine. There is no more pretension.

It cannot happen overnight. Those who say they are changed instantly don't know the meaning of change. Experience is different from words. When you sit in meditation, you become your own *guru*. *Gu* means "darkness" and *ru* means "remover"—you become the remover of your darkness.

Deepening Meditation: Who Am I?

So first relax and allow your body to relax. See your pleasant face and tell your mind you are taking some time for yourself. Then you feel *veerum* on your breath and build the rhythm of your breath within you. Slow down and then do *hrim* and let the energy come up. The energy, which was accumulated and engaged at the lower level to satisfy the lower desires, is lifted upward. Your attention is raised to higher levels.

Then you are ready to begin to use the mantram *kohum*. *Ko* means "who" and *hum* means "I." To remove pretension, ask *kohum*, "Who am I?" Very gently and slowly with a relaxed feeling, you ask this question. Probe into yourself. It is an investigation, a confrontation with yourself. Try to see who you really are. Ask yourself if you are what others think you are. Examine what *you* think you are. See if that is not a projection of what you *want* to be. Ask, "Why do I want to be that? Is it my idea or someone else's?" If you are trying to mold yourself according to someone else, are you free? Is living like this bringing you true understanding of life?

Then you repeat *kohum*. Let the investigation within

yourself continue. Don't repeat it over and over without pausing to ruminate. Tell the mind to come here and find out who you are.

Man's mind can take him everywhere. You may be sitting for meditation and your mind will take you to the Eiffel Tower for tea. It also takes you around your own environment: do you have the right job? the clothes you like? the right place to live? The mind drags you through all your different hangups and feelings.

You must ask, "For what am I living? Is there really happiness in the things I live for or am I putting the happiness in?" Objects don't hold happiness. You put your happiness in them. It is a sugar coating which you have applied, it is your imagination. Because of your imagination the things appear sweet, without it they appear bland. When you go into *kohum* meditation, you are not just imagining, you are knowing.

Two things happen in this meditation. In the first stage your mind will investigate. When it becomes tired, it will become calm, quiet; it will give up the race. This is the second stage, when you are able to reach your real Self. To be with yourself is bliss.

When your mind starts working for someone else, worrying about the job or the boss or an old friend, or longing for something you don't have, then say *kohum*. Who am I? I want to be with myself under all circumstances. Whatever comes, let it come. You are open for beautiful gifts. If they don't come, it does not upset you. Still you are you. You are not shutting off the world of friends, but you are not always craving or running after things and you are not unhappy because you don't get those things.

You begin watching every moment. You don't let anyone disturb your peace. You watch so that your words don't disturb anyone else. Watch so that no one takes your precious time in vain and you don't waste anyone else's time. Don't allow anyone to put negative thoughts in you and watch so that you do not put negative thoughts in anyone else.

Meditation makes you so aware of yourself that you feel your own words; you hear the sound, the tone, the gesture, the impact. If you hear that your tone is harsh, ask yourself: "If someone spoke to me that way, would I like it?" That person is a human being. You are creating pain for someone. Do you have some human feeling for the other person?

With this approach our relations become sweet. Many friends will come to you because they will see that your eyes, words, feelings and actions are very peaceful. They will see that when someone tries to hurt you, you don't take notice. You say, "I don't want your abuse," and you leave it behind.

This way your whole life changes. You become true to yourself, you have no pretension. If you don't like something, you have the right to say, "No, I don't like this." But you say it politely and gently, not in a curt way. There is no need to be a hypocrite; simply say, "Thank you, but for me it does not build harmony or peace." Your words are not harsh because they are not in reaction.

Deepening Meditation: Eliminating Negative Traits

Start the day with the mantram, asking, "Who am I?" In the evening you look again and see everything that happened in your day. If all was harmonious, be glad and feel your peace. If any upsetting incident arose, don't judge yourself. See it clearly and rectify it in your meditation. You are building a new life.

The second mantram we use this week along with *kohum* is *nahum*. *Na* means "not" and *hum* means "I"— "I am not that." To any feeling which is not yours, any experience which is imposed on you by anybody—society, religion, family or geographical conditions—to that you say *nahum,* I am not that, and you erase from the past whatever bothers you. Again and again, say "No, it is not me." In this way, what you are identifying with psychologically will gradually be eliminated. These psychological identifications limit us, or hang us up. It may be an experience from childhood or our adult life, which has caused a scar or fear. To all these we say, "No, this is not me." This is the meaning of *nahum.*

If any fear comes, you think: "No, this has nothing to do with me. Fear is a mental concept. This is not for me." And then in action, you do the thing of which you are afraid and immediately the fear will be over.

Many people die because of fear—of cancer, heart disease or other things. A story will explain what I mean. One day a merchant was walking along a road leading to the city of Baghdad. Before long he met another traveller and they began to walk and talk together. The first

asked the second where he was going and he replied that
he was going to Baghdad also. When asked what his business was there, the traveller said that he was the Plague
and he was going to visit Baghdad and kill many people
there. The first man was amazed and asked the Plague
how many people he would kill in the city. The Plague
told him that he would kill 500 people. As they neared
the city they parted company and went their separate
ways. Then a great wave of sickness struck Baghdad and
eventually 5,000 people died as a result.

Two months later the merchant was leaving the city
to return to his home after finishing his business there.
As he walked along the road, again he met the mysterious
traveller whom he recognized as the Plague. Immediately
he said, "My friend, you lied to me when we talked before." The Plague asked, "What do you mean?" Then
the merchant said, "You told me you would kill only
500 people, but now 5,000 have died of the plague in
Baghdad." "It is true," the Plague replied, "but I did not
lie to you." "What do you mean?" asked the merchant,
"You told me you would only kill 500 people and yet
5,000 have died. How can you say you did not lie?" The
Plague said, "I only killed 500 people. The rest have died
from their fear of the sickness and of dying. I only took
500 lives, the others killed themselves with their own
fears."

When fear takes root in our mind, then the plant can
grow and blossom and bear its fruit of suffering. So now
we say *nahum* and we uproot all our fears before they
can bloom. Again and again you have to deny that this

is you until your mind is convinced. Saying this once, your mind won't be free. You must be a little hard with yourself while you still keep a gentle feeling. It is like a sauna bath—first you take the heat, then you go into cold water, and then back. When you are both hot and cold with your mind, you drop all your past fears.

Now when you say *kohum* you see exactly what you are, without anybody's opinion or projection or conditioning. It may take time, but you will go deeper and deeper until you see yourself exactly. Then you say *nahum* to anything which drags you down, holds you or gives you any negative feeling. Saying *nahum* you throw it out.

Working with these powerful mantras, we go deeper and we relax. Then we find our meditation is gentle and peaceful; we are eliminating all negative feelings and building the good feeling of being ourselves. Working this way for one year, a little each morning and each night, everything will be changed—our business, our family, our friends, the quality of our life and mind—all will be improved. When we change inside, everything around us also changes. Using these mantras, we are learning how to go deeper into the subconscious level, deep into our past where we erase and build anew.

It is never too late. Meditation has the power to start new life from any moment. This way, every day becomes a beautiful dawn to bring in light. We see in *ourselves* that which we are seeking in all the teachers. Every day the sun brings the teacher. *Avatar* means reincarnation; each day brings the reincarnation of the sun. And if you don't see the light in the sun, how can you see the light anywhere else? The sun represents light inside as well as outside. We only need to open ourselves to that light and we will be able to experience joy.

Our purpose in meditation is to enjoy the symphony of life. For that we need three aspects—the hand, the head and the heart, working in harmony. What our hands do must be in our head and what is in our head must shine from our heart. Our body, mind and spirit must be synchronized and work on the same frequency. Then we don't do things in separation; that is, we don't do something with our body which we don't believe in, or something with our mind which our heart opposes. Each day observe how many hours you are able to spend with these three aspects in harmony and synchronization. For this you sit and use the mantras *kohum* and *nahum*.

CHAPTER

V

Meditation: The Art of Life and Experience of Light

Now that you have been studying and meditating, some of your friends may be curious when you mention that you are learning these techniques. Some may support your effort. Some will only listen to you. A few will ask: "Why do you meditate? What is this Oriental way of sitting, closing your eyes and not being active?" Sometimes it becomes difficult for you to answer their questions. To formulate a response or to give them some insight, you must know why you are practicing meditation.

If your reason and purpose become clear, you will continue the journey, and naturally you will convince your friends with your living, with your experience, and with your positive behavior. But if you don't know why you are practicing meditation, then it becomes a fad. Everybody seems to be practicing or talking about meditation. You may try, not because of your conviction, understanding or purpose, but because you have heard and read about it and you want to join the procession. If that is the case, then your practice of meditation is not going to last very long. It is not going to help you because you are not convinced from inside. It is not going to bring a positive change in your life because you have not understood the purpose of meditation.

First we get a glimpse of the ideas behind meditation. Then we go further into the practice of meditation. When we experience meditation, the change in our lives will stir the curiosity in friends. Our conviction may cause a change in their lives. Then they may help another friend as one lamp brings light to another lamp. In this way the process of peace, happiness and growth goes on increasing in a circle of contribution.

First, let us see what benefits we get from meditation. Our life now is full of tensions which have come from all directions. We grow up under pressure which builds like a pyramid. When we are young, the pressure comes from our parents and our teachers. We were compelled to read books, to take our examinations, to receive credits and make our grades. Even before school, we felt pressure from our parents and society. Generally they used a negative approach. Rather than teaching by their own example, they would say: "Don't do this, don't do that." Our energy would not remain quiet for long, and when we acted independently we were often rebuked.

The tension between your inner energy and the directions you received from the world was built in your childhood. As you grow, your feeling and energy seek to communicate. You try to find some partner, some friend, some comrade with whom you can converse and exchange feel-ings. In this quest you will find a tug-of-war of jealousy and competition for affection. The mind, instead of com-municating, becomes a watchdog. "Who is my friend with now?" it asks. Inside you experience jealousy, competi-tion and a burning sensation when you know that your friend is a friend to somebody else. You are not able to live comfortably, but you are not able to let it go. In this conflict the pressure builds.

When you are a little older, you begin the search for employment and decide how to earn your living. There also, competition and pressure are created. Before you go for an audition or job interview, you know how much ten-sion you build inside. When you fail at an interview you become depressed. You start rejecting and neglecting your-self, thinking, "I am worthless." Instead of seeing the situa-tion as it is, you start blaming yourself. You start seeing worthlessness in yourself and you go so far down that psy-chological tension builds up in you. Old sayings of your childhood and old thoughts come to your mind. Yes, your father or mother told you that you are nothing, or your teacher or neighbor criticized you. Because you did not get the job, you start believing that these old thoughts were right, that you are wrong, and you begin to doubt your self-worth.

These are all the psychological, emotional and social tensions that accumulate around your consciousness. When you reach adulthood, you have additional prob-lems and anxiety from your spouse and your children. You feel obligated to keep your family happy. You always

have to be at your best to see that they enjoy a happy
mood. If you don't, there is friction and demands from
your children or from your partner. Then you have your
emotional needs to gratify, to release all this accumulation
of tension. Your brain and mind are working under this
constant tension.

Our brain is composed of fine tiny nerves which are
bearing intense pressure. The tension is like a wrestler or
boxer, jumping and bouncing on a baby's stomach. You
can imagine what would happen. This is the situation for
our brain nerves. Still, we survive. The biggest miracle is
that we withstand the pressures created by present conditions.

Many people don't recognize that they have problems.
They can hide their neurotic emotions and attitudes with
money, parties, meetings, eating and running from activity
to activity as a kind of drug. There are so many ways to
cover yourself. Yet the neurotic attitude remains underneath. The aim of meditation is to cure this underlying
neurotic attitude.

How do we cure ourselves? The first step is to calm
yourself. It is the same as using the brake on your car.
You know there is a puncture in the tire, and it is unsafe
to continue. You take your car aside to see which tire has
the puncture. Many drivers don't notice until an accident
takes place, until they are hospitalized. They may have
a heart attack, high blood pressure, diabetes or ulcers.
They go on running until one day their doctor diagnoses
the physical manifestation of their inner condition. From
where did the ulcer come? The person did not notice the

puncture until it became an ulcer, causing a severe accident.

In the same way you sometimes see that something is uneven in you. Observe whether your body is calm or anxious. If you are calm, your breathing will be flowing naturally and you will be able to relax. But if you are not calm, you will feel restlessness even while you are sleeping. You will roll and toss in bed. Why don't you enjoy your sleep? All of nature's creatures enjoy sleep with the exception of people. Your lack of that simple enjoyment indicates something is wrong. The evening hours are meant for quiet, night is meant for rest. At night when you don't rest, this indicates that something is accumulated in your body. Your bed is filled with accumulated tension.

Review

In meditation you are deliberately making an effort to overcome this condition. You watch yourself using the methods we have discussed and you relax each part of your body. Slowly you learn the art of relaxing with your awareness and attention. Then visualize yourself, become your own observer. See your face, your nose, your chin, your hands, how you are sitting. Many people are drooping, walking around with their heads down, afraid and ashamed. They do not use their spine properly and turn their faces upward in a natural way. Our face is meant to look toward the sun, stars and moon. Man is the only creature whose face naturally looks upward; all the animals look only downward or at best straight ahead. As human beings we have gained the upward glance. If we cast our faces down, we are not able to see anything or anyone eye to eye.

If you watch yourself and are pleased with yourself, you are pleased with the world. When you are not pleased with yourself, you hide from people. You won't look directly into their eyes, because you can't look directly into your own eyes. If you know how to look into your own eyes directly, then you are able to do the same with everyone. The main conviction you need is for your own self. You don't need to convince anybody else. You don't want to prove anything to the world. You have tried for so many years to do that without any success. Now in meditation, you are looking inward. You are observing yourself, stepping back, stepping out and seeing yourself. This is a basic part of meditation.

Next watch your breath and begin to count your inhalation and exhalation. You take a deep breath and your whole body becomes like a balloon with fresh oxygen. Each cell must get the touch of this fresh breath. If you keep a window partly open, a little fresh air comes. It should not be too much of a draft, however; just a very smooth, gentle current cooling you down. Then you do "hrim" several times and raise your energy upward. Then you use the mantram. Inhale with "vee" and exhale with "rum"; come with "vee" and go with "rum." Experience the beautiful rhythm of your breath. Or you can use "so" while inhaling and "hum" with exhaling. You develop a slow steady rhythm which relaxes your tension and enables you to wear a natural smile.

Meditation and the Art of Communication

Your friends will begin to notice the change in you. They will think: "What is this something new in him?" You are wearing something beautiful; as you wear perfume, good clothes or ornaments, now you are becoming inner-poised. You are not in a hurry to voice your opinion. You are able to listen; you have patience so that when your friends want to say something, you are ready to listen to them. Previously you were intervening in their conversations. Before they were finished you would interrupt to state your opinion. Now you are not the same person. You say, "I am not in a hurry. Let the person be ready to hear me. If the person is not ready, my words are not so cheap to be wasted by voicing them when they will not be heard." Now we don't value our words. We go on popping them out whether the person is listening or not. We speak so fast that before the person digests the words, another sentence springs out from us. We don't allow any time for them to digest what we say. Even when you pour something into a bottle, you have to pour it slowly or it will overflow or miss the bottle. This is the new approach in your life.

You also know another secret—how to encourage the person to listen to your words and your feelings. How? The best way is to empty that person first. Then you can pour your own thoughts in. That is the art. But if you go on pouring before the person has emptied, it will overflow and what you have poured will be lost. This meditation teaches you to be patient. It gives you insight to listen. When that person knows that he has told you what he wanted to say, he gets a kind of satisfaction. With that degree of contentment, in that happy mood, whatever you say goes directly in and stays. You have also had the time to think more exactly, and to gauge the mood of the person. Once you know his or her mood, you may say exactly what you want to say. You will have the last word.

In this way meditation helps you to build a beautiful communication, conversation and communion. Your friends will notice the change in you and ask you about the cause. You will be a new person, and they will try to be like you, instead of you being like them. It should not be an obsession to make others like you, but it is your happiness to share what you have received, like perfume, with others. You share this new experience of poise and people will like it.

When you have broken the pattern of tension, you are in tune with your breath and you have insight. A new philosophy of life has come to you. You recognize that you are not this or that byproduct of the society in which you are living. Your real self is that which is happy, flowing, natural and communicating. The tension, the hurry, the resentment is not you, but old conditioning that is eroding. You feel *sohum*—that you are the real self, and you enjoy that instinctive inner happiness that is your true nature.

Now you see through the façade you have become accustomed to wearing. You say, "Inside I am beautiful." That philosophy will make you a different person. You will have some inner sight, inner light, inner awareness and inner strength. You still live in the world, but with a different awareness. When any tension or pressure from society comes near you, you know how to duck and let the pressure go overhead. When you are swimming in the ocean, you know how to flow with the water so the waves do not drown you. If you become stiff the wave will over-turn you. The rush of water pressure will somersault you. If you become flexible, pliable, then you are moving with the flow. Meditation is much the same. You become flexi-ble and flowing. The inside stiffness is gone. You should meditate on this process. You are experiencing how to make life more patient, flowing, calm and creative with-out tension. You are learning how to live. We learn the art of living, that is meditation.

Guided Meditation: Experiencing Light and Life

We are now ready to practice another meditation. We are learning to experience the flow of energy in our body from toe to head. We are seeking to be completely flowing and balanced. This meditation can be done in three ways. In the first method, you read through this section of the book and note the techniques used. Then you may men-tally repeat the process and experience the meditation. Second, some may find it effective to tape record the guided instructions and play them back during the meditation. Finally, you may do this meditation with a partner or group in which one person acts as the guide and takes the others through the meditation.

The purpose of this meditation is to experience the flow of light which is moving in your body and to enable

you to realize your real nature. If you practice this meditation, you will be able to heal your body with this light,
with this concentration and with this awareness. Before
you start this meditation, you have to put yourself in a
completely flowing mood and feel all the parts of your
body relax. You select your posture, either sitting or lying
down, close your eyes, and relax completely. The methods
described in the earlier chapters of this book will help you
achieve this. As you are guided through your body and
each part is mentioned, you must try to visualize light in
that part. As you feel that light is slowly and gently moving
in your body you will have a deep experience of peace and
a deep experience of healing. You will realize there is a
beautiful positive energy which is engulfing you, soothing
you and giving you a unique gentle touch which is full of
healing and peacefulness.

*Now concentrate on your toes. See the light around
your toes, beautiful white light. You will see a thin line of
light around your toes. This light is your real self, your
real energy. It is in the form of light. Now this light energy
is moving near your ankles so you can visualize both your
feet illumined with light. The energy has now come to
your ankles. It is circulating around your ankles and you
feel a pleasant feeling in your toes, your feet and your
ankles. This light is moving upward in your calves. You
see the whole area from your ankles to your knees is nothing but light. See the beautiful pleasant color of the light.
It is yellowish-white. You feel this light moving from your
knees to your thighs. The whole area is being filled with
this light and you don't see your thigh but you see only*

*light. Now from toe to thigh, the whole area is nothing
but light. It is a column of light. Now this light is moving
upward near your pelvis and moving slowly toward your
stomach and navel. The light is slowly spreading, giving a
soothing touch, healing and creating deep, deep peace, in
your abdomen and in your intestines. The whole area is
nothing but light and this is coming slowly toward your
heart. Your heartbeats are rhythmical. You are experiencing a very peaceful feeling. The heartbeats are in such a
gentle rhythm that you feel each beat as a gentle touch,
healing any heart problem. Wherever this light touches
there is no disease. It is spreading, moving slowly and
gently like water up the spine and around your back. You
see this light around your breast, and coming through your
lungs to your arms, in both arms, in your elbows, and
descending into your wrists and fingers. The light is around
your fingers. A beautiful line of light is around your fingers and thumbs. It is a very thin light, a very thin line of
light around your fingers and thumbs. You experience all
the light rays coming in your arms and hands like healing
energy. Slowly you see that both arms are nothing but
columns of light. The light is moving in your throat, and
around your neck. Relax your throat area so the light can
move upward. Yes. You can feel it now, moving through
your throat and voice box. In your mouth, you can see it
on the tip of your tongue, it is pulsating on the tip of your
tongue. It is going gently into your nostrils, your nose and
spreading into your ears. Yes, even in the ears. It is not
stagnant, it is moving. Now you can see it going into your
eyes, and you can see pleasant balls of light in the sockets*

of your eyes. You feel you can cure any eye problem with this light, and you feel the healing touch of this beautiful light. You feel the light moving and soothing your head. You feel it on your forehead, in the center of your brows like a third eye, and the third eye is opening. Now you see it on top of your head. All the brain nerves and brain cells are lit with this beautiful light. All these cells have become animated. You see and feel this living touch throughout your brain. Each brain cell is lit like a tiny bulb. Be with your light, this is you. This is your real self. You see your spine; it is like a beautiful column of light, straight inside and out. From the top of your head, you see your whole body surrounded with light. Your whole body is nothing but light. It is the embodiment of light. You see yourself as the presence of light. You are nothing but light. Experience this light deeply. Become completely one with this light. You are here to experience yourself for the first time as the presence of light. You are completely relaxed. Your body is healed with this touch of light and the flow of light is streaming in your body. This stream of light is flowing and you feel buoyant and very light. Now when you have fully experienced this light, you can open your eyes gently with a pleasant feeling because you have seen this spreading positive energy. You have experienced deep peace. You have experienced yourself as light. Gently open your eyes in your own time. When you open them, look at the people and things around you with a new fresh smile. You can share your experience. How do you feel? Share this positive experience. In that way others will benefit from what you have received in this meditation.

CHAPTER

VI

Meditation in Jain Philosophy

This is a beautiful time, and a unique occasion to meet souls who are on the path to find their own light and their own Self. When we meet such people who are sincerely seeking, from without to within, it becomes a moment of communication and bliss, a time of unity and union.

Today I am going to speak from the Jain point of view on the ways of meditation. Jainism comes from the word *"Jina,"* which means "he or she who has conquered his or her inner enemies." Not outside enemies, but inner enemies. Instead of wasting time conquering outside enemies, wise people use their time conquering inner enemies. When you conquer your inner enemies you rule the world without any army, without any weapon. The whole world is with you because your weapons are compassion and love.

Mahavira was the last prophet, teacher and master in the line of twenty-four Tirthankaras of Jainism. A Tir-

thankara is a great sage or seer, one who builds bridges
among men. Mahavira and Buddha were contemporaries,
Mahavira being twelve years older. Both were princes and
both worked in the same area which is known as Magadh
in the north of India. Mahavira was a *Jina;* he conquered
himself. For twelve and one half years he observed silence.
He did not teach during that time because as long as he
had not experienced the supreme realization, he was not
eager to teach. It is not easy to control the desire to voice
your opinions; for that we need the practice of silence.

Mahavira became Jina. Those who are eager to follow
the path of conquering their inner enemies are known as
Jaina. Jaina is not any religion, any sect, or any kind of
fold. It is a way of living, thinking and practice. Any person who follows non-violence, who has relativity in thinking, and who knows the invisible vibrations of the karmas,
is Jain. Mahatma Gandhi, the Father of modern India and
a Hindu by birth, followed the message of non-violence
and brought this insight into the political movement. He
once wrote "Though I was not born as a Jain, I am more
than a Jain." There is no baptism, no ceremony, no ritual.
By your practice and your life you are a Jain. The whole
emphasis of this philosophy is not on any outside ritual,
but on inside investigation, awareness, transformation.

Meditation requires sincere, serious, consistent and
constant awareness. Real meditation cannot be "instant
meditation." Yes, after long practice, in an instant you go
into meditation. That can happen, but the person must
have some previous background, some former experience.

When I entered the monkhood, for five years I practiced silence. I wanted to know the secret of words, the mystery of life, and what is beyond death. When you observe silence, in the beginning you feel uncomfortable, because you have the habit of voicing your opinions, speaking and making noise. But when you observe silence for a long time, you are not ready to break it when the time comes. The peace is so deep in you that you enjoy being silent. Your eyes are open, your ears are open, you are open to the universe. You are listening to everything, and the noiseless sound.

Silence plays a great role in the path of meditation. At the same time we need inner awareness. Jainism is a path, not a circle; it is moving in a particular direction. That direction is inward, not outward. It is not going anywhere outside. It is finding yourself in being.

This is the first idea of Jainism. In this search there is no boundary between East and West. The boundaries are of the mind, not of souls. We see human life everywhere, pulsating with eagerness, and having a deep inner quest. All souls are equal. If you only see the outer garb you will see that some have white skin, some have red skin, some have black skin. These are all outside appearances. Inside, the flame is the same. This is the real essence of Jainism. This message, which permeated the Indian air two thousand five hundred years ago, is here today.

What is meditation in Jain thinking? Meditation starts with this idea: turn off your outer activity for a while in order to enter the complementary, receptive mood of your soul. Because you are always active, you are busy living outside. You are making yourself empty, and you are not fulfilling yourself inside. Without the inner touch your words become empty, your language becomes meaningless, and your talk becomes only a kind of chatter.

Whatever activity you do, you don't really do it on your own initiative. You follow the herd and act the way many others are acting. The time comes when a person is mechanical in movement, without knowing why he or she is doing or saying something. In order to receive, you must turn off all this activity.

What do you do then? First you sit quietly. You take an *asana,* or posture. It is called *kayotsarga,* which means that you forget for awhile the body and its tension. You allow the body to relax in its own way, like a piece of sponge. So the tension which you have accumulated begins slowly dropping down. *Kai* means the body, and *utsarga* means to drop. Drop your body. Why? Because as long as there is tension in the body, you won't be able to experience the flow of life.

Do you know how much tension you have? Even as you prepare to meet a person, you are building tension in your body and mind. How to greet? How to meet? How to speak? What to say? In this way, in school, in colleges, in our studies, in our society, in our contacts with people—everywhere there is tension. This tension is built in now. Even if you sit for meditation, your body is not quiet. It is jerking. Even though people may sit quietly, they go on biting their nails. They make many gestures because there is no calmness. The first step is to drop your body—allow it to live in its own state. When you have done *kayotsarga,* then you can turn to the mind and the breath.

When you are under tension, you take shallow breaths.

But when you allow the body to flow, the breath goes deep, and you take in proper oxygen. Your body is animated when it is filled deeply with fresh oxygen. The cells are not dead or stagnant, there is no inertia. You need fresh breath. That is why meditation generally was observed on mountaintops, in forests, near rivers, on shores, in the natural environment. As you take in fresh air, your mind is also blossoming. You are opening, and you feel the freshness of your mind.

You become attentive to your breath and begin a mental count to four to bring yourself in tune with your breathing. You use the mantram *hrim* to raise your energy for meditation.

Then, after attending to the breath, you may use the mantram *veerum* to engage your mind. For a long time your mind has been rushing among so many activities, it does not know what to do. The five senses are sending demands to the mind and it is off in many directions.

In meditation you locate your mind in one place. That is why we use mantras. When you breathe in, you use *vee*. When you breathe out, you use *rum*. *Veerum* means to be brave enough to accept the real nature of yourself. This may seem contradictory. You may ask, "To accept the nature of yourself you have to be brave?" Yes. To enjoy your blissfulness, to know your inner thought, and to be in a relaxed mood, you need bravery, because your mind is loaded with worry, anxiety, fear and negativities.

As soon as something beautiful happens we are afraid. We are afraid to embrace happiness. A student recently came and she told me, "For six days I have been feeling joy. Now I don't know what terrible thing may happen to me. When I am so happy and it lasts for six days, I worry that something is going to happen. I don't know what, but I feel it."

The mind is not ready to enjoy blissfulness, the *Sat, Chit* and *Ananda*. These three qualities are in us, but we don't believe that. We have doubt. We believe only for awhile, on the word level. It will be a great day for you when you believe that "This is *my* nature, to be happy, blissful, full of knowledge and immortal. I am *Sat, Chit, Ananda*." *Sat* means immortal. *Chit* means consciousness. *Ananda* means bliss. These qualities are within us—this is what we have forgotten.

We doubt these gifts are for us, as though they belonged only to certain blessed and higher souls. We say, "Oh, Christ was the Son of God; Mahavira was fortunate because he was born in that time. The Buddha was lucky, he was enlightened. But me—don't think of me. How am I to enjoy that?" We don't have faith that this is our birthright, our real quality.

We use the mantras to quiet and engage the mind. In deep meditation, after practice, the time comes when we leave behind all the rituals and the mantras, and go free. This state is called *dharma sanyasa*. That comes when you are free from the shackles of the mind, free from the bondage of desires. Then you need nothing.

As long as the imprints of our longings are set in our mind, we are bound with the shackles of cravings and we are always comparing ourselves with somebody. This is the business of mind.

Using mantras we go inside for the first time. We experience deep calm. When that glimpse comes, you know you have really reached the state of meditation. Then you feel "I am here."

There are three stages as we go inward. In the first stage, your mind is reciting a mantram, but at the same time it is bringing many distractions. Then we use the word *Kohum. Ko* means "who" and *hum* means "I." "Who am I?" You ask yourself this question. Without knowing yourself, you will not reach yourself. It is our real Self we have forgotten.

Slowly put this mantram to your mind, saying: "Kohum." Then the answer comes: "I am form. I am body. I am he or she." Your name comes. Your emotions come. Passion comes. You say, "No. This is not me. My name was given after I was born. Somebody has given me this name. What was I before then?" Then the answer is "the body." But before the body, you were there. You entered the body. Who was it that entered the body? The body is constantly changing. Your body now is composed of completely different cells than your body as an infant. You are going deeper now. *Kohum.*

Constantly you keep removing the layers. When you remove the layers of an onion the freshness comes out. When you remove the layers of a cabbage the fresher leaves come out. The outer leaves are tough and rotten. We also have many psychological layers we have mistaken for ourselves. Because of these layers we become depressed, suppressed, prejudiced, angry, irritated and unhappy. Think of yourself. How are you using your day? Most of the time we are lost in all these layers. We hardly have time to feel our real nature and experience the inner divinity. We use *kohum* in order to investigate our real self, and we go deeper and deeper and deeper.

Three students came to study with a Master. One was a prince, another was the son of a very wealthy sheriff, the third was a humble seeker. They all sat before the Master. The Master asked a question. "Who are you?" The prince smiled and answered "Don't you know me? I am a prince. I am the son of the king." "Oh," said the Master. "You are the prince? Very glad to see you."

Then he asked the next, "Who are you?" The young man replied, "I am the son of the sheriff. And this big garden in which you are sitting belongs to my father." And the Master said, "Oh, I am very glad to see such important people." Then he asked the third stranger, "Who are you?" He answered: "Sir, had I known who I am, I would not have come here. I don't know. That's why I am here."

The Master asked for a little milk, and put some yogurt culture in it. Then he asked the humble student to take this milk and put it aside for twelve hours. It became yogurt. Then he asked him to churn it and he made butter. Then the Master said, "Put the butter on a low fire and make *ghee*." * The student made *ghee,* and then the Master said, "See, this *ghee* was hidden in the milk, but if you had put your hand in the milk, you would not have found it there. This is the process of your growth. You have to add culture, and then allow yourself to be calm. Then you have to churn inside and put yourself on the fire. Then finally the purest substance comes out."

This story sheds light on the nature of our journey.

* Clarified, purified butter.

First you have to put a real message of the Master in your life. Culture means the right knowledge, the right insight. If wrong concepts enter your head, they will cover all your thinking, and you will become lost. Right teaching is as important as right food, right air and right living. Do not follow the herd or hold any belief merely because your father did. You have to be a seeker. Really speaking, life is meant for the truth—to seek and to find it. Don't be stagnant and don't follow anything blindly. Blind faith is not the answer—it may stop your search, become a barrier that keeps you from going further. Awareness keeps you alert, removing all your layers.

In this story, once the culture was added, the Master did not shake the milk, he allowed it to be calm. When you have taken the culture of right understanding inside, you sit and meditate and see for yourself how it works for you. Each individual is unique, so don't compare yourself with anybody. Mahavira's teaching was essentially this: You are an individual light, you are you. You cannot be anybody else. If you compare, you will bring misery and pain to yourself. You are not like anybody else. Your vibrations are with you. If you seek yourself and go within yourself, then you will find you and experience your real nature.

For that we must practice the teaching inside. That requires peace, tranquillity, calmness. That is why you select some calm spot for meditation. Your inside movement will slowly settle down. When you take hot water and put tea in it, the tea settles as it brings color to the water. In the same way, the truth must settle. There is no need to be in a hurry to go to the world and make everybody spiritual. That is a kind of mania. You must practice first. How can you help anyone unless you grow and feel a change and then reveal it through your life? The life of the Master, the life of the teacher, becomes a direct experience. It is beyond words. You see the light, and you follow the message.

In meditation, these teachings go inside and permeate your consciousness; the consciousness which was covered and filled with worry, anxiety, hang-ups and problems from the past is freed. When you become calm, you take the teaching deeper and deeper. Then a process of churning takes place. That is introspection.

In introspection you watch yourself. Let your past come before you, and go on discarding it. You remain in the present. If the past wants to come, let it come and go before your eyes. It is erasing from the tape. When everything is erased, your tape is clean. You have to erase from your consciousness all those past blocks which are disturbing your dreams and your thoughts, causing your anxiety.

You are sitting *here,* not going into the past. Live in the now, here. Allow the past to go before your eyes. This is mental meditation. It is churning. The time comes when you are clean. The period comes when you feel the flame and that outer covering has gone. It depends on your intensity, your steadiness, your calmness, your introspection.

When the butter is churned, you have to put it on the fire to clarify it. Fire is called *tapa.* In any life some kind of *tapa,* some austerity, penance, or a little suffering is involved. There is no growth without some kind of giving.

In *tapa,* you are purifying yourself, as gold is purified in fire. In the same way, our soul is purified by giving. And when this cleanliness comes, your soul becomes pure like *ghee.*

In the same way, you will know what you are. The inquiry meditation is *kohum,* "Who am I?" To erase negativity and outer layers we have the second mantram *nahum,* "I am not this." And the third mantram in this meditation becomes *sohum,* "I am that." When you become clarified, you know *sohum,* your real Self, "I am I."

This is the process of meditation, which gradually brings you to experience your Self. You may use these three mantras which are used by the Jains to investigate and reach the *sohum* state of bliss.

Meditation is used in order to reach your higher Self— that is its purpose. In meditation, you raise your lower self to the higher Self, and enjoy the state of *sohum.* This is the message and meaning of meditation, and the Jain way of thinking, living and being.

CHAPTER
VII

Sense Beyond the Senses

We all have to be more open in our lives. We are caught up in social conventions and trivial thoughts, trapped by lust and desire, confined in our minds. That is why our vision is limited. And the purpose of life, our mission, is to develop our potential fully. Unfortunately, generations of walls have been built up around us—cultural, social, sometimes religious barriers which prevent us from stretching out and reaching beyond prescribed boundaries.

Our situation is like that of a caged lion, fighting to escape, full of strength, energy and vigor. When he begins his struggle to get out, he finds the bars too strong, and his energy becomes dissipated. He loses his power. Eventually he succumbs, accepts his defeat, surrenders to the environment, and lives like a small helpless creature. With the passing of time, he forgets that he is a lion.

This has happened to us. The soul of the human being

is fire and light. It has strength. We not only have a potential to develop physical power, but we also have an inner spiritual strength which has to be nourished and sustained as well. It is always said that we need material possessions, material accomplishments, and a position in life in order to survive on that level, but we need to tend the soul too, in order to survive as a totally fulfilled individual. Then life becomes a series of beautiful meetings in the universe. While we live, we live happily. And when we leave, we leave with peace. We understand the importance of this philosophy when we see that for purely materialistic people, both living and leaving involves unhappiness. They live with difficulty, depression and fear of defeat. When the time comes for leaving, they are sad and fearful, and they go from the world without any awareness.

There is an extra sense, beyond the five natural senses: to touch, taste, smell, see and hear. It is a spiritual sense, a sixth sense, which gives meaning to the other senses. Without this sixth sense, the senses are senseless. When people look, they do not realize what they are seeing. When they listen, they do not understand what they are hearing. When they talk, they do not know what they are saying, and sometimes, mean, unkind words come popping out. When they touch, they do not grasp what they are feeling. When they taste, they do not recognize fully what they are eating. All this happens because they have not developed that extra sense which adds true sense to the senses. That is why we often talk about senseless conversation, senseless observation, senseless living. When you develop your sixth sense, life becomes full of meaning. Then we say—"That person is sensible." When "sensible" is used in this way, it means "aware." Every moment, this person knows what he is doing; every hour he knows what he is going to do. He feels actions before they occur because his sixth sense tells him. This sense is in full working order, not rusted, disused and neglected. It is shining like the sun. And when this inner sense shines like the sun, the whole world is bright.

Why do you enjoy the day? Because there are no clouds blocking the sun. When there are clouds hiding the sun, the day is dull, everything appears gray and gloomy. You do not feel like going out or doing anything, so you sit indoors drinking coffee and wasting energy. When the sun is bright, you want to go out. You cannot help yourself; something draws you out. You feel alive! In the same way, when your sixth sense, the extra sense, is shining, you feel joy in life. You do a small thing, and the act itself gives you a touch of joy. Even if you shake hands with somebody, you feel a real communication of two lives. If you look at a small flower, it stimulates your communication with the life force. You see life growing, pulsating and blossoming. The intrinsic tenderness of life diffuses the fragrance and color. Even a single flower can give you illumination. You do not look upon the flower as a common object and thoughtlessly throw it away. You establish communication between life and life. When you sit on the grass, you feel the same thing. You are delicately communicating with inner life, and you are growing.

As the shell of an egg is broken and life comes out, in the same way the shell of ignorance is broken and something intelligent emerges. Unfortunately, many people never break through this shell; they die without ever being properly born. Only when you make the real breakthrough, see and relate to the universe with the extra sense, can you feel and experience real life.

There is a word in Jain philosophy for this sense: *pragna*. In other schools, it is called the third eye or higher consciousness. There are many different words for that special awareness, *pragna*. With *pragna* you break through ignorance, your perception is different. Things dawn on you. Everything you see becomes a means to joy, because your inner mechanism has changed gear—turning all it sees into joy. That is the art. The artist who paints a still life and transmits a living quality onto his or her canvas has this inner sense of perception. This is really ESP. It is not just reading someone's mind, or having a premonition about who is coming to see you. All these are ephemeral phenomena, merely telepathic, child's play, and happen when the mind is becoming clear. You are waiting for some mail, and the next day the mailman delivers the mail you were thinking about. Your mind wanders to a person you have not seen for a month, and you go out on the street and bump into that person. You daydream and a certain face comes into your head and after a week that same face is introduced to you for the first time. All these things do happen. But these are just *indicators* of a strength and potential we all have within us. We have to go further, to develop this inner power so that everything in life hums with happiness, peace and serenity.

Then the essence in you will welcome any challenge.

You will think: "Here I am, let anything come. I have the art of heart to transform all things and bring balance." Take this challenge now, from today, and work on it. Say to yourself: "Let me use my extra sense, my inner sense, my wisdom and intelligence to turn every event into joy, into understanding, into creativity." It is a challenge. Take it up. Try only for a year and see. The wisdom of *pragna* will dawn upon you.

This extra sense requires constant use to make it work properly. If you break a hand and it is in plaster for a month, when the cast is removed and you try to stretch your hand, you will not be able to do so. Your hand has become useless. To bring it back to proper working order, you have to massage and exercise it every day for several days. Then the hand will do things for you. In the same way, people who do not use this extra sense will find it has become numb. In fact, for most people, it is so numb that they do not think they possess it. They say, "The masters have it, but we don't." They accept that they are lesser mortals and try and make do without it. I call this *spiritual bankruptcy*—not to realize, understand and feel the inner intelligence which is the essence of this universe.

Great teachers do not take pleasure in people worshipping them; they are not on this earth to respond to flattery. Words of praise mean nothing to them. They exist to show mankind that *pragna* is the birthright of each soul, that we all have this strength inside, that we have to exercise it. It may take some time and patience. If you use your broken hand too quickly and try to force it, you may break it again and be back where you started. You bring it into action slowly and gradually. We must treat this inner energy in the same way.

In the morning and in the evening, put aside some time to be alone for a while. The journey to the unknown is always made alone. You cannot go with a crowd. When you are alone, in communication with yourself, ask: "Who am I? What is my pattern and mechanism? Am I manufacturing unhappiness every day or do I have some inner art to transform unpleasant events into pleasantness? Do I have that art? If not, why don't I? Who or what stops my progress?"

The lesson to be learned here is this: that you do not attribute this lack of happiness to another person, blaming your mother, father, teacher or somebody else. Do not rest at that conclusion. Truly, it hurts you when you settle for the belief that another person is the cause of your unhappiness. You are not really analyzing the situation, facing up to the reality. You are rationalizing *out* true understanding. You must make an effort within yourself to break your own barrier of negativism. Be positive and say, "I want to be happy today anyway. I am not going to spoil my day because of somebody else. I cannot afford to waste a single day. Each hour is precious and meaningful." In reality, each day that you receive is a blessing.

In the morning, start with this: sit and concentrate on yourself. Feel and believe: "There is *pragna* inside me and I shall exercise it. I shall limber it up, take it with me and use it throughout my day, in the office, in my work, in the bus or on the subway, with all my coworkers, friends and companions. Also whenever someone throws negative vibrations toward me, I will burn them up and turn them into positive constructive energy." It is a very significant decision which takes much courage to make. But with your extra sense, you can conquer your inner enemies. Then you will find that your outer enemies will no longer be a trouble. When you have this inner awareness, outside influences cease to be a limiting factor. Your attitude converts them into positive elements. This metamorphosis is not achieved through intellectual gymnastics. It is done wholly through awareness, meeting all aspects of life and making them beautiful, using your extra sense to give sense to the senses and to all things.

From now on, let us move in the world, radiating our Self wherever we go. Let us realize that our journey on this planet is to experience our Essence. Let us all understand the intrinsic meaning of this extraperceptive sense and celebrate life with enthusiasm.

CHAPTER
VIII

Perfection Is in Us

Perfection is in us. Completeness does not come from outside. To find that inner perfection you have to tune into it, then you can experience and enjoy the harmony inside. If completeness comes from outside, it is borrowed. It is not yours and will not last; it will not remain permanently, perpetually, eternally. Only that which is yours will remain permanently. That is the universal law.

You have to bring out your perfection; to do so you have to be aware of your energy. You have to use it to move in the right direction. To turn on the radio, you get up and turn the proper switch. If you stay seated in your chair and just think of turning it on, it is not going to start. In life also, we must move to bring out what is in us. Through meditation you are seeking to turn on your own radio so that your inner power can come out. Your personal music will be heard and amplified.

Take the analogy of the diamond. No jeweler can give

it the quality to sparkle. By being polished, each facet reflects light. Then the rough diamond begins to look like a
real gem and everyone appreciates it. If you put a rough
diamond in a ring, no one will believe that it is a diamond.
They will wonder why you have put a common stone in
your ring.

We are all like rough diamonds. If you polish a diamond and bring its innate quality out, it shines. If you
polish your soul and remove all its impurities, gradually
its innate quality of light is revealed and that light becomes a guide for further light. One door opens another
door, and that door opens another.

Today we are going to meditate on completeness and
fulfillment and the wholeness of life. What is completeness? Let us think of what we want in this life. Have you
any thoughts about it? If you have, please share your ideas,
your dreams with everyone.

*(The audience responded with these comments: "To be
happy." "To be free." "Contribute to the evolution of man
and build a new society." "Fearlessness." "Love.")*

Let us examine your thoughts. You say "to be happy."
Everyone wants to be happy. Have you ever heard anyone
say that he wants to be unhappy? Even those who have a
tendency to feel unhappy are also seeking happiness in
their unhappiness. In psychology, it is called masochism:
to become unhappy in order to be happy. Even here, the
goal is happiness in a way.

You say "to be free." How can you be happy unless
you are free? If you are not free you are not in a condition
to enjoy happiness. A slave cannot enjoy happiness because

of the restrictions on him. In order to be happy, you have to be liberated. You want freedom, but if you have fear, how can you become free? See how all these desires are connected with each other. You say different words, but there is a common source underneath. In order to be happy, we have to be free, and when we are free from fear, then we may enjoy freedom.

How can you have freedom unless the society you live in is healthy? In a narrow, unhealthy society, people around you are negative. Their standards are low in all aspects—commercially, physically, financially, intellectually and spiritually. You cannot remain aloof, so you have to do your part to change the society. In a healthy society you have freedom, you have fearlessness, you have happiness. And to build that society you need love.

If you don't have love, you can't work for somebody. What you do solely for money isn't real work. At your office, you wait for the clock to show "five," and you hurry out. Here there is only a financial binding, no love. The mother does not tell the child she will not change his diaper past a certain hour of the day. No one pays her a salary. The relationship between a mother and child is one of love. She would remain hungry to feed her child. She would not care for herself; she would lose her sleep, everything, in order to make her baby happy.

Have we a mother's heart for the whole world, and do we work with the same zeal, the same feeling, the same love? If you can give this love, you will not criticize someone behind his back; you will lovingly try to correct mistakes. We need this kind of love in our life. This love is not only intellectual, but it is a feeling on the spiritual level. I call this love "faith in action." We have to understand how we can radiate this kind of love toward the society in which we live. We must not think, "I'm happy, why should I worry for the world?" We must know that if the society is not a happy one, we will not be happy. Sooner or later, the prevailing unhappiness is going to affect us all.

You might have heard the story of a lonely woman who was ill with an infection. A physician warned the village sheriff that if she were not treated with medicine, the disease would spread. No one took the doctor's advice or cared for her and gradually her body became so infected that she died. By now the germs which had killed her had spread all over the neighborhood. An epidemic broke out. In each household, someone contracted the disease. When the woman was alive, she was despised and ignored, but when she died, all the townspeople became her partners and shareholders in the illness! The story warns us that if you don't help a person in distress, ultimately you are going to fall victim to the same problem.

We meditate and know how we can become happy, free, fearless, loving, and how we can rebuild society. The first thing we have to know is where happiness comes from. Do you think happiness comes from the accumulation of wealth or a whirl of social activities, or from name and fame? If inside there is sadness, if inside there is burning, if inside you are upset, you may move among society's elite, have name and fame and riches, but you won't be happy. You must get to the core of the problem. You are starting from the outside, but really you must start from the inside. If you are happy within, you won't care for name, fame and other extravagant things. If they come, let them come; if they don't, let it be. I've seen happy people with few possessions, and I have seen people with a lot of possessions always dejected, brooding, and worrying about their problems. People who are happy are in touch with themselves. First of all, we have to have a connection with our own selves. That is the main thing. In this materialistic society, the most lonely and forlorn person is the materialist himself, because he does not have insight into spiritual life or inner power. He does not have a sense of these inner values. He has limited himself and lives in a narrow world. When you go inside and make the connection with your own self, you are happy even with a few things. If more things come, they will add to your happiness if you have inner awareness. But if you don't have inner awareness, your material things can pile up and still there will be a void, an emptiness. The material things will fail to bring you joy.

We see here how to have the inside touch. When you sit for meditation, concentrate on your energy. Feel each part of your body. "These are fingers, these are arms, this is my head, here the whole body is vibrant." Because of "something," all these limbs are active. Go on concentrating and observing to see what this "something" is. "My body touches, my tongue tastes, my nose smells, my eyes see, my ears hear and my brain thinks." Why is it that sometimes eyes are there but don't see, ears are there but don't hear, tongue is there but can't taste, skin is there but does not feel, and brain is there but can't think? With this inductive affirmative and deductive negative questioning, you will go inside and come to one conclusion: that it is your soul that makes your body work, and because of it your senses sense, your limbs move and you communicate. And when the soul leaves, the body starts to decay. Then the corpse becomes an object of fear. It is the same body which was loved, but when the soul has left, no one wants to be alone with it even for one night. It is now only a lifeless corpse and no one wants to have contact with a dead thing. Without the soul, we don't want the body.

We have been giving first preference to the body. Now when we see soul, we start giving first preference to soul. But we do not neglect the body. The combination of soul and body makes life. A materialistic man gives first preference to the body and knows nothing of soul. A spiritual individual sees the spirit and uses the body to support his spiritual growth. Then the body becomes a temple. He uses words, mind and senses to produce beautiful music. Every hour of the day there will be music if one is aware of one's soul.

When you are connected with your soul, bad thoughts and negative feelings won't arise. Your soul will remind you and tell you something is wrong. When you get that kind of advice, you won't think of doing the same thing again. Your soul is your best friend.

A spiritual person is always aware of his thinking. Worthless thoughts are not part of the composition of his life. Being in tune with everything, we can make our life a garden. We cannot live without thoughts, but we must be selective. If you want to make a beautiful garden, you have to select seeds, flowers and bushes and arrange them thoughtfully. In the same way, let your mind select the thoughts you want. Once someone told me he did not have control over his thoughts. I asked him if he owned his brain or someone else's brain. If it is your apartment, do any worthless people enter without your permission? If it is your brain, how can unwanted thoughts come into your head without your permission? You have to realize this. Tell yourself, "I will not let any thoughts come in without my permission because I am the master of my mind, my brain."

To question every thought that comes to your mind requires complete awareness, and to be aware, you must exist in the present. If you are not in the present, unwanted thoughts will come in. That is why all teachers say: "Be Now Here. . . ." If you are somewhere else, either in the dead memory of the past or in the fantasy of the future, it is as if wandering thoughts know and see the open door and walk in. Once they take possession of your brain, they are difficult to drive out. One needs a lot of effort to get rid of them. Thoughts which have penetrated deeply become like old tenants. They don't leave willingly. You may not like them, but they are not going to leave you. If you watch your thoughts and live in the present, your life will become different; your mind will be like a garden. Love your thoughts as flowers, and you will make progress. You have to love yourself, fall in love with your own thoughts. When you can say, "I love my thoughts, they are beautiful, they are like gems to me," when you have that kind of awareness, then every string you touch on the sitar of your mind will create melody. Life will sing with harmony.

Watch each word that comes from your mouth, because it comes from your thinking. See whether it is a healthy, beautiful word or a foul one. If you want to understand the psychology of a man, listen to his words and conversation for one or two days. They will reveal what is inside. The thoughts are the mother, and the words are children. Children often resemble the mother.

Now consider action. Action is last because it shows the inside desire or outside longing. According to our thoughts and words, our behavior follows. Behavior is nothing but a byproduct of thought. You may compel a person not to be violent, and he may sit calmly, but you cannot stop the inner turmoil. Once Mahavira told King Shrenik that even the king could not stop the butcher Kalchowrik, who killed 500 bullocks every day, from killing animals. The king took up the challenge and said that he could stop the butcher for twenty-four hours. Then he sent for the butcher, put him in a basket, and had him lowered into a dry well so that he wouldn't get a chance to kill anything. The next day, the king told Mahavira that the biggest butcher in the land had not killed anything for a whole day. Mahavira smiled and asked the king to ask the butcher what he had been doing while he was in the well. The king put the question to the butcher, and the butcher answered that he had been killing oxen in the well. He said that he had made an ox out of clay at the foot of the well and chopped off its head saying, "One is killed." He had made another and had said, "Two are killed." In this manner, he had passed the day. "What else could I do in the well?" he asked. It was a game; but the game involved emotion, so it was true to life. Mahavira told the king and the others: "If you don't change a man's thought pattern, you can't change his action pattern."

If you change yourself by external actions and your thoughts are the same, there will be no change in you. That is why nothing is greater than meditation. In meditation you are in tune with yourself, with your own music, with everything that you are doing and thinking. You bring change in your life from inside to outside. The outside change without the inside change can only be temporary. But when you come to your center and start watching yourself, then your progress starts. To do this there are three kinds of meditation.

The first is observation of your thoughts, called "surfacing." To use an analogy, you are sitting in your apartment at a window from which you have a commanding view of the street. Observe the street from your position. Cars and trucks and people keep coming and going. Everything is passing, but it doesn't bother you because you are on the third floor and are just watching the whole street. The traffic and people are coming and going. Suddenly you spot an acquaintance or friend in the crowd and your attention focuses on that person. Up to now, your attention was on the whole street and you did not pay keen attention to any particular thing. If you had paid too much attention to the traffic you would not have been able to have peace of mind. So you just let the traffic come and go and you remain uninvolved. But now if your friend is there in the crowd, your attention is drawn there. What do you do? You send someone down to ask him to come up. Your friend comes up and you sit and talk together while the traffic moves below. Occasionally, your eye falls on the traffic, but your conversation goes on. You are in tune with one another. Let the traffic pass. In this type of meditation, you let the traffic of your thoughts pass, let it come and go at the back of your mind. Many things are buried inside us. When you were not aware, as a child in school, or in your business life, many thoughts went deep into your subconscious and still lie buried or hidden there. When you sit for meditation, you will notice that thoughts will come. When you are busy, thoughts don't come, but when you sit quietly, they come rushing. That is the first sign that you are becoming aware of them. The thoughts are always there but only come to the surface because you are still. Let the traffic come and let it pass. Don't pay heed to it. All of a sudden you find a good thought, an inspiration, and you catch it. Be one with it. When you are in tune with that beautiful inspiring thought, other lower thoughts will automatically pass by. Meditation with something pleasant is the first way. Something beautiful comes to the surface and you are in tune with it while other things pass. Hidden thoughts will come out and you will feel an unusual lightness and buoyancy.

Another way of meditating is to choose an object or idea to which you respond with feeling: a flower, the moon, a beautiful picture, a calm statue, or peacefulness. Looking at the flower, you notice that it is beautiful; there must be a sense of beauty in you because you see that beauty. If you don't have the sense of beauty within you, how can you see the visible token of beauty? The flower is fragrant and there is something in you which enjoys its fragrance. By connecting yourself with the flower, you feel the universal connection. You are not alone. You are connected with the universe and you can see and feel oneness with the flower, the plant, the moon, or anything you have selected to focus your attention on. Or, if you take an idea, go with it and see its correspondence within you.

In the third type of meditation you concentrate on your breath. Your breath is your life. You can live without most things, but you cannot live without breath. You can fast for a long time, but you cannot stop breathing for even ten minutes. With closed eyes, concentrate and flow along with your breath and gradually go inside. There will be times when you are completely in tune with yourself. In that peace, you will find unity of body, mind, spirit and universe. Everything becomes one. You feel whole: no pieces, no fragments, no compartments; the fullness of yourself is complete unity.

According to your disposition and according to your need, inclination and metabolism, you may select one of these three suggestions to glide into meditation.

CHAPTER

IX

Realize What You Are

When a bucket has even a single hole in it, no matter how many times you lower it into the well, the water will run out. What about the mind? Nature is there continually offering all its innumerable gifts. But if the mind has holes in it, how can it retain what it receives? No matter how many times it is filled with the bounty of the universe, it still feels lack and emptiness.

What makes these holes in our thinking? It is our many barriers, boundaries, likes, dislikes, resentments, judgments, expectations, projections, in one word, our karmas. Nature has no discrimination. The sun, the rain are for all. The air we breathe is universal; all are breathing universal breath. In our hurry to give labels and categories to the world, we do not see its beauty. We do not feel our feeling. We pass by nature's bountiful offerings.

How to fill up the holes of the mind? *Paushadha*—take time to retreat from the many activities which have created wounds in your psyche and mind and heal yourself. Take a few hours, a few days, a few weeks to heal yourself with the deep all-pervading peace of meditation.

Many of us do not know that we are bleeding inside. We have put bandages on top of our wounds to absorb the bleeding or we have taken outside medicines to dull the pain and numb the limbs. What kind of bandages do we use? Small entertainments, a myriad of activities to keep us busy. As long as we are young and healthy, we don't notice the way we have been using these "painkillers" as a crutch.

The time comes when the downward spiral begins. The symptoms start to show. Inside there is hollowness, brooding, weakness, fatigue. The time comes when we have to confront ourselves. The time comes when we have to see our pain and call a halt to running away from it. *Praktikramana*—Step back and see what you are.

The real enlightened souls, from past and present, from all different geographical locations, used their days and nights for introspection, understanding and meditation. Their inner voices took the form of words, and from these utterances of pure ecstasy and insight we glean wisdom. Out of their deep compassion for mankind they shared their teachings with us to inspire and uplift our lives.

What did they see? The indiscriminative Sentient Energy which is blissful, beautiful and immortal, hidden in all living forms. What did they understand? That the universe works like a calculator, totalling all of our vibrations. Each thought we have has its own vibration. According to the way it vibrates in the universe, it attracts subtle atoms. These atoms are what build our thinking, speaking, longing. Thus the ancient wise people were able to diagnose man's disease. They found that pain does not come from without, but comes as a result of something within our own negative vibrations.

There are three steps we can take in order to fill in the gaps of mind and make ourselves whole: (1) realize, (2) recover, and (3) retain.

First, realize what you are—the microcosm of the macrocosm. Before you can see the invisible, start with the visible; before you experience the formless, investigate the forms. See that in form you are composed of the same elements as the universe. The solid parts of your body—hair, teeth, skin, nails and bones—are the earth elements. They are the "dust." All the fluids—blood, sweat, saliva, tears—are the watery elements in us. That which causes chemical reactions, including the digestion of food and body heat, is the fire element. The breath which is constantly coming and going is the air element.

So what is without is within. There is no running away from the world. The form you see in you is the form of the cosmos. In ancient Jain palm leaf manuscripts, artists even depicted the form of the cosmos in the form of man.

Because of this deep relation between microcosm and macrocosm, we are affected by seasonal changes. If it is cold outside, our body feels cold. Just as nature's forms are in a constant state of flux and change, so our form is undergoing continuous change.

What is the hidden reason for change? What is the law

behind the cycle of the seasons? To renew and refresh. In order to remain continually fresh, water is ever-moving, ever-renewed by the ebb and flow of the tides. Like water, if life does not flow, it becomes stagnant.

In order to adjust to the laws of nature, all forms accept change. We can learn even from the trees. In the fall, they give up their leaves. They do not resist. It is a process, a catharsis, a fasting, a cleansing, a shedding. It is throwing away the old in order to make room for the new. There is no sorrow or pain. There is deep patience. There is deep wisdom. They know that the life force is retained. Heat remains in their roots.

The trees know: "If I want new leaves, I have to give up old ones." Similarly, if you want to feel fresh and make room for the new, *let there be a fall in every season of your life.* Drop away old thoughts like dry leaves and open yourself to new ways of thinking and living. If you want to expand and grow, keep your relationship with the universe continually positive, receptive, expectant.

At the heart of Eastern philosophy is the teaching of detachment. What is this philosophy? It is merely a philosophy of the seasons. It is learning to live in harmony with the seasons. It means this: the things which are relevant to this moment in time are relevant, and the things which are not relevant to this moment are not relevant. Holding on when it is not relevant to hold on—that is called attachment.

When you are clinging, you don't know whether things are relevant or not. Clinging makes you do one of two things, either feel remorse when the attachment goes, or drain yourself trying to hold what cannot be held. When someone or something goes, allow the passage. Flow with the seasons.

One who is detached gives up with reverence. Like the leaves which dance as they give themselves up, you give up with joy. To receive is joy. Everyone likes to receive something new. To give up with the same joy is very difficult.

And yet if you don't give up, you don't receive. Continuously there is giving and receiving. When you give up with balance, tears don't cloud your vision. When you give up with poise, you don't feel inside pain and regret. When a person leaves you, say "I wish you well." Holding on or regretting, you are losing both the person and your peace. In return you are getting nothing but the results of your negative vibrations.

To realize what you are, meditate on the philosophy of life which can help you change your old habits of mind. Say to yourself, "All right, the trees give up. Why do I not?" Watch each thought. Ask yourself, "Is this thought living in the past?" If so, then you know that you are not living in harmony with the season. If you notice that your mind likes to escape into the barn of old memories, say to yourself, "I am going out of the cycle of life because I am living in the past. The past has already given me the result I wanted and still I am clinging to it."

By watching you are able to untie yourself. You resolve, "I want to go further." Many good things are waiting for you tomorrow if you untie yourself from the past. All the springs come from winter. What you call barren-

ness is to the trees nothing but a period in which they
have to wait in expectation. This period is given to you
for your understanding.

It is a period of transition, before the coming of spring,
before the rebirth of new life. In reality there is no death.
We are like the baby nursing at the breast. When the
mother notices that milk has dried up on one side, she
moves the baby to the other side. In between, the baby
cries. He does not see that in between is the moment of
awaiting the new fresh milk. He does not see that there is
no real loss.

By watching you are able to see how old habits of
thinking disconnect you from your here and now and
make you unhappy. Are you projecting the concept of father
figure, husband, wife, or other image onto another person?
If so, then you do not see that individual as an individual.
Are you comparing the present moment with the past? If
so, the freshness of life is not enjoyed. You go on missing
good feelings, deep communication. And people get bored
with you because you always bring out the old imprints of
mind, the worn-out things. Then you find someone with
the same problem as you and you wallow together, drag-
ging each other down.

The philosophy of vibrations changes your whole life
style. Your level of consciousness ultimately attracts people
from the same level of consciousness as your own. So you
have to raise your consciousness. New life cannot come
only from words. It must come from new thinking, new
vibrations.

To bring those new vibrations, drop the old, clear your

files, throw away junk. Say to yourself, "I don't want those old thoughts, those negative memories, those conditionings." When you go on clearing, your mind becomes light. But before they go for good, the past imprints will tempt you and play tricks on you. If you are not careful, they will keep on giving flickering signs to you and they may make new scars on your consciousness.

You must not allow them to make you angry and frustrated. You must talk to them and tell them, "Now you go! You are old tenants and your lease is up! I will not renew your contract." Once you recognize that these so-called tenants are unwanted guests, then you are ready to evict them. You realize that you must have invited them into your consciousness long ago when you were in a hazy, ignorant state of mind. Old habits of thinking know how to make themselves at home, but no matter how comfortable or comforting they may appear to you, you must be firm in your resolve to empty your mental house.

If this sentient living energy does not give up the old insentient, the stale stagnant matter becomes a burden to you and a cause of pain. The more thorough the mental housecleaning, the more buoyant you feel. The more you allow dry leaves to drop away, the more aware you are of what you are in essence and of what is relevant to your present living. Now you are open to receive the new.

What is the new life? None other than that living conscious energy pulsating and vibrating in the entire universe. It is your own latent power. To enter the path of meditation you must have a conscious awareness of your latent power. If you are not aware of that treasure within you, you are not going to long for it. You are not going to reach for it. If we see the end in the beginning, we will take the beginning to the end.

For that you must believe in yourself. Until now you have believed in everybody but yourself. Now you must realize that you are holding a precious diamond within you. Polish it and your radiance comes out. Otherwise it remains like a rough stone, covered with so many layers. You must say to yourself, "Just now I am a rough diamond, but I have confidence that inside me is brilliance. Inside me is latent power. I want to get in touch with that in me."

When you have this confidence, you really work on yourself. You *upanishad*—sit close. Sit close to whom? To yourself. Or to him or her who can take you to yourself. To the "diamond-cutter" who knows just where to cut so that your roughness is broken and the whole diamond comes out. The teacher is not always one who wears the clothes of a guru. The guru is anyone or anything who removes the darkness of your ignorance, who helps you uncover your brilliance. Once you uncover your Self, you become your own teacher.

Once there was a king who used to lead a life of self-indulgence. One evening he was sitting on his balcony at dusk. The sunset was particularly striking and the king was moved. It was the rainy season and the sunset produced the full spectrum of seven colors. The king became so happy that he continued to watch eagerly.

Slowly he saw the colors fade away; darkness came over everything. He saw the dark and he realized in a flash, "O, is this not my life? I am pulsating with pleasures. How long will this sunset remain? O, let me be aware before my colors disappear. The painter must paint the scene while the colors are still vivid or the moment is gone. Can I not do something worthwhile with my life before it is too late?"

The king became so deeply aware of his inner consciousness that he put an end to his former self-indulgent ways. The sunset so inspired him to see his own true quality, that he transformed his life. In this story the sunset was his guru.

Meditation is this: a complete transformation of consciousness, an uncovering of that universal indestructible energy which lies hidden in you. Otherwise you can sit and recite a mantram to get calm, but it will only be a temporary balm. You will return to the rat race unchanged.

Removing the tenacious, covering layers of the mind, you get in touch with the latent Sentient Energy which gives life to form. If it can give life, then it cannot be captured by form. If it could be captured by form, then it could not be formless. The formless remains above the forms. That is why it can give life to them.

There is a beautiful story in the *Upanishads* in which a son came home to his father after twelve years of study telling him, "O Father, I have studied all the scriptures and experimented in all ways, but still I did not find Soul." His father then asked him to break open the fruit of the banyan tree and show him where the tree could be found in the thousands of seeds living inside the fruit.

The son answered: "O Father, that which gives birth to the tree cannot be seen."

"Yes," said his father, "And the power which gives life

to you cannot be measured by any instrument. Atma, Soul is beyond. That which gives life to all the forms is intangible. Yet it gives force to the tangible world. It animates all the seen forms. That energy is you. That energy is me."

When you realize this, you will discover the purpose of meditation: to get in touch with that Formless in you. The insight comes that this vibrant conscious energy has been covered up by your own negativities. So covered, it does not get light or fresh air.

This discovery leads you from the step of (1) realizing what you are to (2) recovering yourself. Just as you recover your health after realizing that the cause of your illness is in you, so you recover your natural energy when you become aware of the layers which cover you. You will see that sadness, depression, anger, greed, pride and deceitfulness are all outside coverings. They are not natural to you. They have stifled your natural latent power.

The process of recovery is a consistent and persistent practice. It is a continuous throwing off of the covers to get fresh air. It is getting a fresh connection with your flow of inner strength. That is meditation. It is not instant.

We must work at recovering, little by little, so that we return to our original nature. Once we have opened the wounds of our psyche to the fresh air and light, we must take care that they heal properly and completely. We must seal up the gaps and doubts of mind by filling ourselves with positive vibrations.

Without realizing, we cannot recover. And without recovering fully, we cannot go on to the third step: Retain. In order to retain, let us flood the mind with the light of meditation and fill in the holes in our thinking with knowledge, understanding and experience.

Say to yourself, "I am the microcosm of the macrocosm. As the universe moves I must move. In the universe there is a pulsating element. In the heart of all the forms, all the cells, in my own form, there is some vibrating life. That is my real nature. I want to recover my original nature and bring out my natural qualities of blissfulness, peace and conscious vibrant energy hidden at the center of myself."

Once you are confident beyond the shadow of a doubt that within you is a universe of beauty and truth, energy and bliss, you will be able to retain. With the light of awareness permanently shining, you will retain the universal blessings which are yours.